Careers for You Series

MCGRAW-HILL'S

CAREERS FOR

PEOPLE

ON THE MOVE

& Other Road Warriors

MARJORIE EBERTS
MARGARET GISLER

SECOND EDITION

New York Chicago San Francisco Lisbon London Madrid Mexico City
Milan New Delhi San Juan Seoul Singapore Sydney Toronto

The *McGraw·Hill* Companies

Library of Congress Cataloging-in-Publication Data

Eberts, Marjorie.
    Careers for people on the move and other road warriors / by Marjorie Eberts
and Margaret Gisler — 2nd ed.
        p.   cm. — (McGraw-Hill careers for you series)
        ISBN 0-07-149317-4 (alk. paper)
        1. Vocational guidance.   2. Motor vehicle driving—Vocational guidance.
I. Gisler, Margaret. II. Title. III. Title: People on the move & other road
warriors. IV. Title: People on the move and other road warriors.

HF5382.E233 2008
331.702—dc22   2008004424

1 2 3 4 5 6 7 8 9 10 11 12 13 14 15 16 17 18 19   DOC/DOC 0 9 8

ISBN 978-0-07-149317-8
MHID   0-07-149317-4

McGraw-Hill books are available at special quantity discounts to use as premiums
and sales promotions or for use in corporate training programs. To contact a
representative, please visit the Contact Us pages at www.mhprofessional.com.

This book is printed on acid-free paper.

· ·

To the road warriors in our families
who are always on the move—
Marvin, Martha, Tony, Les,
Maria, Ann, Mark, and David

Contents

CHAPTER ONE

Job Opportunities for People on the Move

G et behind the wheel in the United States, and you can travel on more than 2.6 million miles of paved road. Then, if you want to rough it, there are more than 1.3 million miles of unpaved roads. Cross the border into Canada, and there are 875,000 more miles of road to travel. All along these roads, there are people and businesses needing a wide variety of goods and services that can only be delivered to them by trucks, cars, buses, taxis, vans, limousines, and other vehicles. The career possibilities are endless for those who would like a job that truly keeps them on the move. You could be delivering mail along a rural or suburban route. You could be transporting children on a school bus. You could be bringing produce from farms to processing plants. You could be moving furniture across the country or bringing gasoline to local service stations. You could be patrolling highways. Just drive along any road and look at all the different vehicles. You will see thousands of road warriors who have found careers that let them spend their days behind the wheel. There are wonderful career opportunities out there for you, too.

The Special Attributes of Road Warriors

You know that you truly savor every moment that you spend behind the wheel. Did your love of driving start back when you were just a child driving toy vehicles? Did you look forward eagerly to getting a learner's permit to drive as a teen? Is your idea of a dream career the opportunity to spend your workdays on the move? Finally, is your love of driving backed up by the right set of skills to succeed in a career in which your workplace will be streets, roads, and highways? Answer the following questions to see whether or not you have the common characteristics of road warriors whose careers keep them on the move.

1. Are you safety conscious? Companies want drivers who avoid having accidents.
2. Are you willing to follow safety rules? All jobs on the road require strict adherence to safety regulations.
3. Do you have the stamina to do physically demanding work? Many jobs on the road require considerable lifting.
4. Can you pass a demanding physical examination? Many drivers have to pass a complete physical examination every two years.
5. Are you willing to drive in such adverse conditions as rain, sleet, and icy roads? Many driving jobs regularly present these challenges.
6. Are you patient? Many days will be spent in traffic jams.
7. Are you flexible? Many jobs require you to handle a variety of responsibilities.
8. Can you handle stress? Other drivers on the road may not follow safety rules and may even display road rage.
9. Are you able to work alone? In many driving jobs, you will be the only person in the vehicle.
10. Are you willing to work different shifts? This is often a requirement. You may have to drive at night.
11. Are you willing to get additional training? Many driving jobs require special training and/or continuous education.
12. Do you have solid communication skills? Taxi and bus drivers spend considerable time interacting with riders.

13. Can you work effectively without direct supervision? Drivers usually only have contact with their supervisors by radio.
14. Are you willing to spend days or weeks away from your home? Neither long-haul truckers nor traveling salespeople are at home every night.
15. Are you comfortable with technology? Driving jobs these days often involve the use of computers and other high-tech equipment.

Finding Your Dream Job

This book is designed to help road warriors like you find the perfect job. You'll learn about jobs that let you drive around in your community, throughout your state or province, across country, or between the United States and Canada. Here is an overview of some of the jobs that you will read about in this book. One of them may be just right for you.

Driving Taxis, Vans, and Limousines

If you want a career that will let you work in your community and at the same time stay on the move throughout your workday, consider a career driving a taxi, van, or limousine. Of course, you will need to have a good driving record plus the ability to locate little-known streets and find the quickest route to a destination. It also helps if you truly enjoy people, for each trip will bring you in touch with different personalities, from frenzied parents taking a child to the hospital emergency room to tourists eager to sample the cuisine of a well-known restaurant. You may even find yourself driving celebrities, from screen stars to sports figures. This career will also give you the opportunity to choose between working for a company or owning and operating your own vehicle. No matter which of these choices you make, the key to financial success in this career lies in the number of individuals you drive to their destinations each day.

Driving Local Trucks

One of the occupations slated for the largest job growth through 2014 is driving local trucks. This career gives you the opportunity to drive a wide range of vehicles, from eighteen-wheelers to pickup trucks. You can also drive very specialized trucks, such as dry-bulk carriers and tank trucks. No matter what type of local truck you drive, you are likely to be involved in some way in its loading and unloading, even if it is only to direct helpers. Your days can be set if you drive a fixed route to make prearranged deliveries or pick up products. Or every day can mean driving to different locations. If you have a special talent for sales, you can not only drive a truck locally but also sell the product you carry. One of the special benefits of choosing a career as a local truck driver is that you are able to come home each day.

Driving Long-Haul Trucks

Long-haul or over-the-road truck drivers lead a very different life from those in most careers—even local drivers. They are typically away from their homes for a week or more at a time, and then they spend just a few days at home before going out on the road again. For some long-haul drivers, their trucks become their only residences, and they live full-time in their comfortable cabs, which are now often like mini-apartments. Some companies use two drivers on very long runs. One drives while the other sleeps, and stops are only made for fuel, food, showers, loading, and unloading. Many of these driver teams are husband and wife. While some long-haul drivers follow the same route on every trip, many must go where they are sent by dispatchers to pick up and drop off all kinds of freight. When these drivers start a trip, they rarely know the places they will go or how long they will be gone. The lure of the open road and the camaraderie of fellow truck drivers make this career attractive.

Driving Buses

Choosing a career as a bus driver involves having far more than good driving skills—you must be able to deal with passengers. If you drive a local or intercity bus, you can expect to collect fares, announce stops, and answer all kinds of questions, including the perennial "When will we get there?" As a school bus driver, you must make sure that all the students are sitting in their seats, treating each other with respect, and entering and exiting the bus in a safe manner. Motor coach drivers who take people on charter and sightseeing trips must closely follow the planned schedule as well as work with tour guides to make the trip comfortable for all the passengers. They also may be gone from home a week or more at a time. Besides keeping all the passengers safe and happy, bus drivers must often deal with heavy traffic and poor weather conditions, so this can be a very stressful job.

Driving for Delivery Services

A steady stream of delivery people brings letters, packages, and products to homes and businesses every day. What's more, they bring them fast—perhaps even overnight. And they also bring them by vans, trucks, and smaller vehicles, which makes these jobs perfect for those who want to be on the move throughout the day. Plus, you have a choice of employers, from the United States Postal Service to local, regional, national, and international delivery companies. No matter where you work, you will need to know every street on your route or service area and be an efficient sorter who can arrange everything that you are delivering in the order that it will be delivered.

Driving Emergency and Public Safety Vehicles

Drivers of emergency and public safety vehicles drive vehicles with flashing lights and blaring sirens as they hurry to the scenes of emergencies. They may drive fire trucks, police cars, or ambulances. Besides needing to have excellent driving skills, many of these drivers are certified or licensed emergency medical technicians or paramedics. In this career, you provide a valuable service to others—you may even save lives. Another career opportunity within this area is working as an animal control officer with the responsibility of protecting the health and safety of humans and animals.

Teaching Others to Drive

It takes training to be a safe driver, whether you are a teenager, a truck driver, or even a racer at a track. While most driving instructors are not behind the wheel for most of the day, they are definitely on the move. The greatest number of instructor positions are at driving schools, teaching beginning drivers the secrets of parallel parking, entering and exiting freeways, and just driving safely. You don't have to have nerves of steel for this job, but you do have to be a very skilled driver with a knack for teaching, especially working with teenagers. Truckers driving the large tractor-trailers as well as bigger straight trucks are required by federal law to get a commercial driver's license. Truck driving schools have programs that help them earn this license and get the training in driving these big rigs that both trucking and insurance companies want their drivers to have. For the extremely skilled driver, there is also the possibility of teaching racing techniques, stunt driving, and high-performance driving at driving schools such as the Bondurant School and the Jim Russell Racing School.

More Jobs Behind the Wheel

When you think of what type of job lets you be on the move throughout the day, you may think only of such traditional jobs as bus, truck, limousine, or taxi driver or as delivery person. Many other careers offer you the opportunity to be in a motor vehicle and on the move for most of the workday. These careers, however, may not be thought of primarily as driving careers. The list of careers that will put you in the driver's seat also includes race car driver, parking lot attendant, heavy-equipment operator, wide-load warning driver, realtor, traveling salesperson, meter reader, and armored truck driver, as well as all the other drivers that you observe doing their jobs as they travel down the road.

How to Become a Road Warrior

Companies will not hire you just because you want to spend your days behind the wheels of a motor vehicle. They will expect you to demonstrate solid driving skills as well as other skills that are essential to excelling at a driving job. For most of these jobs, an ability to handle paperwork efficiently is necessary. Some jobs require excellent communication skills.

Most driving jobs only require graduation from high school or the equivalent. However, you must obtain special licenses to work at many of these jobs. This can be done most easily by attending a driving school.

The better you can drive, read maps, handle paperwork, and use a computer, the better prepared you will be for a driving career. Those of you who land the very best jobs will often have had some previous work experience.

Choosing the Right Career

Choosing a career that lets you be on the move is only the first step. You also have to make a choice from among the many career possibilities within this broad category. Answering the following questions can make this decision easier:

1. Do you prefer to be at home every night? Some careers, such as long-haul truck drivers and race car drivers, require long absences from home.
2. Do you mind working shifts? Police patrol officers, firefighters, paramedics, and taxi and bus drivers typically have to work shifts.
3. Would you like to do a lot of overtime work? Many of the careers that will keep you on the move also require long workdays. Postal carriers, police patrol officers, and delivery workers can have almost as much overtime as they wish.

4. Would you like to combine staying on the move with another career? Realtors, traveling salespeople, and emergency road service operators have this option.

Looking for a Job

The traditional ways of obtaining jobs work well for road warriors. If you are anxious to work in your community, read the want ads in your local newspapers and visit local job websites. If you wish to venture to another area, visit the websites of associations in the career area that interests you. These sites have employment information for jobs across the United States and in Canada. You can also get leads from friends who have driving jobs. Visit state and provincial employment offices, too. And in today's Internet world, many jobs can be found by visiting company websites, as well as sites that post job listings for multiple companies.

CHAPTER TWO

Driving Taxis, Vans, and Limousines

D rivers of taxis, limousines, and vans are on the move day and night. They have the important job of getting people to their destinations quickly and safely. People who don't have a car, can't drive, or aren't able to take a bus depend on taxi, limo, or van drivers to get them to meetings or medical appointments. Business travelers need drivers to take them to the airport, hotel, or work. Other people want to be transported to leisure activities like the theater, dinner, shopping, or a concert.

New York, Chicago, and other large cities have many taxis, limousines, and passenger vans. Even smaller cities and towns have companies that provide personal transportation. If you want to meet new people every day and drive them to their destinations, being a taxi, limousine, or van driver may be the career on the move that is right for you.

Taxicabs in History

Throughout history, people have been in the business of transporting individuals from one place to another. At first, they actually carried them. Remember the movie scenes of Cleopatra entering Rome? From the earliest of times, drivers have also transported individuals in horse-drawn vehicles. It was not, however, until the late 1800s that a motorized vehicle was first used in Paris, France. In the United States, taxicabs first appeared in about 1898. Then, during World War I, taxicabs were used for a very unusual reason: the French used them to transport troops from Paris to the Marne River battlefield. Today, taxicabs are used throughout the world.

The word *taxicab* actually comes from combining and shortening the words *taximeter* and *cabriolet*. The taximeter was a device invented in 1891 by Wilhelm Bruhn to accurately calculate the distance traveled and the resulting fare. The cabriolet was a two-wheeled, horse-drawn carriage often used for hire. Most modern taxicabs still use taximeters to determine fares.

Driving a Taxicab

Driving a taxicab can be a very challenging but rewarding job. Work hours can vary, days can be very long, and customers can sometimes be rude. On the other hand, being behind the wheel all day is a road warrior's dream, and meeting friendly, interesting people is exciting.

Taxi drivers, or cab drivers, usually drive around the streets looking for people who need a ride. Passengers hail (wave down) drivers as they cruise through the streets. This is how taxi drivers get most of their customers. Drivers may also have prearranged pickups in which passengers call the taxi company, give their location, and ask to be picked up at a certain time. The taxi company dispatcher then calls the driver on a radio, cellular phone, or onboard computer to inform the driver about the pickup. Many larger cities have established taxi stands where passengers can wait for a taxi. These taxi stands are commonly located at places where people frequently need a taxi, such as airports, hotels, and train stations.

As a taxi driver, you would probably drive a large four-door car that has been converted for passenger transport. Some taxis are specially equipped to transport disabled passengers or the elderly. These drivers get special training to operate the equipment safely and transport special-needs passengers.

Basic Duties

Once they pick up a passenger, drivers turn on the taximeter to start determining what the fare will be. Sometimes, they need to load luggage or packages for the passenger. When the traffic is heavy or the weather is bad, taxi drivers must be extremely careful not to have or cause an accident. Plus, they must avoid sudden stops or turns that might jar their passengers. It is absolutely essential for cab drivers to be familiar with city streets so they can get the passengers to their destinations quickly. They also must know how to get to commonly requested destinations, such as hotels, convention centers, railroad stations, and airports. Plus, they should be prepared to give recommendations on places to visit and good restaurants. Taxi drivers also need to know the location of hospitals and fire and police stations in case of a passenger emergency.

Once a driver reaches a passenger's destination, he or she must calculate the fare and inform the passenger. Fares often have many parts. The taximeter measures the fare based on the distance traveled and the amount of time the trip took. There may be an added charge for additional passengers, a fee for handling luggage, an after-hours surcharge, or a drop charge. Passengers usually add a tip or gratuity to the fare. The tip is based on how satisfied the passenger is with the driver's service. Then the driver logs all information about the trip on the trip sheet. This information includes where and when the passenger was picked up, the destination, and the total fee for the trip. It is also a record for the taxi company of the driver's activity and efficiency.

Working Conditions

As a taxi driver, your work hours can vary a great deal. Some drivers work full-time with regular hours. Part-time drivers likely have work hours that change from day to day. It isn't unusual for taxi drivers to be called to work on short notice. Full-time taxi drivers usually work one eight- to twelve-hour shift per day. Part-time drivers work half a shift each day, or a full shift one or two times per week. Many taxi companies offer service twenty-four hours a day, so there are drivers on duty day and night. Early morning and late evening shifts are common. Taxi drivers may need to work long shifts during holidays, weekends, or other special events to meet increased demand for taxi service. Traditionally, New Year's Eve is the busiest night of the year. And the busiest times each day are likely to be when the traffic is most congested. Independent drivers are able to set their own hours and schedules.

Being a taxi driver is a very sedentary job, as are most road warrior jobs. However, it is not a solitary job; you will be in the position of spending your time on the job dealing with people. The more successful you are, the more people you will drive each day, and the more varied your experiences will be. You will encounter people with friendly or antagonistic personalities, those who are in a hurry as well as those who are relaxed. From fare to fare, you will adjust to the different demands of your passengers. You may also find yourself in an enclosed space with those wearing too much cologne and some who are inebriated.

Qualifications and Training

You cannot work as a taxi driver without the appropriate licenses. Local governments set the license requirements for taxi drivers, so they vary from city to city. Minimum requirements include having a regular automobile driver's license. It is also necessary to get a chauffeur or taxi driver's license. This usually requires the driver to pass a written exam or complete a training program. Applicants must know motor vehicle laws, safe driving practices, local geography, taxicab regulations, and show some aptitude for customer service.

Canadian taxi drivers must have some secondary education and at least one year of safe driving experience. In addition, they must have a Class G driver's license in Ontario and a Class 4 driver's license elsewhere. Taxi drivers must obtain a municipal permit.

Since taxi drivers have to deal with all kinds of people, you need to be tolerant and patient, even when a customer is rude, to handle this job. Having patience is also important when you are driving in heavy traffic. Because passengers rely on taxi drivers to pick them up on time and get them to their destinations quickly, you must be dependable. And you should also like to talk if you elect to become a taxi driver because there is a lot of talking in this job.

Taxi drivers need to be expert drivers with good driving records. Some taxicab companies offer on-the-job training for their new drivers. They show them how to use the taximeter and communication equipment and how to complete paperwork. New drivers learn about popular sightseeing and entertainment destinations as well as driver safety.

Most taxi drivers pay a fee to a cab company to lease their vehicles. Some buy their own taxis and go into business for themselves. These independent owner-drivers need a special permit to operate their vehicles as a company. An independent driver needs to have good business sense and be responsible as well as self-motivated to be successful. Taking courses in accounting and business can be quite helpful. Knowing how to perform routine maintenance and make repairs can reduce expenses.

Job Outlook and Earnings

Currently there are good opportunities to get a job as a taxi driver in the United States and Canada because many drivers transfer to other occupations or leave the labor force. Opportunities are best for those who have good driving records and are willing to work flexible schedules. You will find the most job openings in metropolitan areas that are experiencing rapid population growth. The number of job openings does fluctuate from month to month and season to season. Extra drivers are frequently hired during holiday and high tourist seasons.

How much you earn as a taxi driver depends on the hours you work, the tips you make, and where you work. Not counting tips, the earnings of taxi drivers vary from about $6.50 per hour to more than $15.00 per hour. Owner-drivers earn from $20,000 to $30,000 per year, including tips. In large metropolitan areas, earnings are usually higher.

On the Job with a Taxi Driver

Jason Pace has been driving a taxi in a suburban community for several years. He got his job because he was a friend of the company owner's son. He first began driving part-time and later, with more experience, started working full-time. Jason drives a minivan rather than the typical car most taxi drivers use. Before he could begin driving a taxi, he had to get a special permit from the city. While this is no longer the case in his state, new drivers do need to be fingerprinted and have a good driving record.

In this job, Jason believes it is helpful to be a good listener and a "minipsychiatrist." It is not unusual for people to share their life histories and all their troubles with him in a fifteen-minute taxi ride. Having a good sense of humor is helpful, too. Jason feels good taxi drivers need to have an even temperament and lots of patience, especially when driving in heavy traffic.

A Typical Day for Jason. Jason begins his day at about 8 A.M. when he turns on his radio in order to get calls from the dispatcher. The taxi is his office, so Jason leaves his radio on all day. He is usually very busy in the morning because he transports many commuters. When Jason first began driving, the heavy traffic during the morning and afternoon commutes really stressed him out. But as he became more experienced, he gained confidence and was able to focus more on customer service and being courteous to his passengers. Because he works on commission and for tips, it is important for him to be efficient, friendly, and helpful with his passengers.

Jason has fewer riders during the late morning and early afternoon. Then he gets busy again as commuters end their workdays and need transportation home. During his day, Jason may make several long hauls to the local airport. Occasionally, he delivers packages for people or companies. His day usually ends between 4 and 5 P.M.

Career Pluses and Minuses. Jason likes driving a taxi because each day is different. It's never routine. Some days he works on the west side of town. Other days he works all over town, or he makes runs to the airport. He doesn't see the same people day after day, although he does have a few regular customers he enjoys transporting. Jason also gets the opportunity to help a lot of elderly passengers, which makes him feel good. Another big plus for Jason is that he earns a very good income driving a taxi.

One negative to this job, according to Jason, is not receiving any benefits. Also, he is displeased that people do not highly regard taxi driving as a career. In addition, he points out there is little opportunity for advancement. And, of course, heavy traffic can be a big problem some days.

The most negative aspect of this job is the risk of robbery. Jason drives only during the day, and his route covers a suburban area, so his risk is not as great as for some other drivers. Nevertheless, he still is very cautious.

On the Move with a Paratransit Driver

Brandon Lockhart drives a taxi for a company that transports people with disabilities and the elderly. He has been driving for this company for five and a half years. His vehicle is a full-size extended van with a high roof. It is equipped with a wheelchair lift, although not all of the company's vans include lifts. Brandon's van has four high-backed seats fitted with shoulder and lap belts and room for two wheelchairs.

A typical day for Brandon begins at 7 A.M., when he picks up his route sheet, which includes scheduled pickups and drop-offs. Next, he goes to the garage area to get his assigned van. He usually has the same van from day to day. The company does have a maintenance crew, but Brandon still likes to check the van over before beginning his day. He always checks the lights, flashers, oil, tires, and fuel. If he sees anything wrong, he reports it to the maintenance crew to be fixed. Very rarely does he find any problems because the overnight crew is thorough and has the van ready for him first thing in the morning. Once he has checked everything on the van, it is time for him to get rolling.

Brandon's Passengers. Brandon has to pick up an elderly woman who has a doctor's appointment at a local hospital. When he arrives at the woman's house, he goes to the door to announce his arrival. Sometimes, he helps passengers put on their coats or carries things for them. He often has to assist them as they climb the three small steps to enter the van. Some of the passengers have a difficult time fastening their seat belts, so Brandon offers his assistance. Once today's first passenger is safely buckled in, he continues to his next stop, where he picks up another person before stopping at the hospital. Again, he helps the passenger get in the van and get buckled into the seat.

At the hospital, Brandon helps his two passengers exit the van and enter the hospital. Sometimes, he helps passengers find out where they need to go for their appointments. Since Brandon regularly takes passengers to the hospital, he knows his way around quite well.

Depending on his schedule, Brandon may wait at the hospital for one of his passengers. At times, he picks up someone already at the hospital who is waiting for a ride. On other occasions, it is back on the road to his next scheduled pickup. Today, his dispatcher has called to give him an address for a pickup that has just called for a ride. The dispatcher knows Brandon is closest to this address because each van is equipped with a tracking device. The device shows Brandon's exact location on a computer in the dispatcher's office. So it's off to his next stop.

A Closer Look at Brandon's Job. Brandon's days are usually busy. He also has days when he and two or three other drivers have very few scheduled stops. They often spend their wait time in the garage area. Since they are on call, they must always be ready to go out on a run. The drivers like sharing stories, taking short naps, and watching some television. Some of the more energetic drivers wash or vacuum their vans. Brandon likes to keep his van looking good because his passengers feel more comfortable in a clean, well-running vehicle. Brandon's day ends between 3 and 4 P.M. He turns his van into the garage crew, who fuels it up for the next driver, who will have it on the road until about 7 P.M. This second-shift driver is almost always a part-time employee.

Brandon first became interested in this job when a family member was temporarily wheelchair bound and needed transportation in a specialty van. He went to the company and applied for a driver position. He had to go through a background check, then Brandon completed a company-sponsored training program that included getting his chauffeur's license. He also learned basic first aid, CPR, and how to operate the wheelchair lift. He had to demonstrate that he was familiar with the city's streets and the location of the city's three hospitals. At first, Brandon only worked on a call-in basis on the evening shift. Several months later, a position opened up on the day shift that was full-time.

Brandon earns an hourly wage and is not allowed to accept tips, but many people like to give him little gifts to show their appreciation for his services. He also gets health insurance, sick leave, and vacation time through the company. The company is currently investigating the possibility of offering a 401(k) plan for its drivers.

Career Pluses and Minuses. What Brandon likes most about this job is being able to help the elderly and disabled and talking with lots of different people every day. The older people have many great stories to tell to someone willing to listen. Because he is a true road warrior, he especially likes being on the road most of the day. Brandon doesn't like bad weather and especially dislikes the first few snowfalls of the winter. He says this is when drivers forget how to drive carefully. Brandon is a very cautious driver, which has paid off because he has never had an accident in his van. As far as passengers go, he doesn't like having complainers who never know when to stop complaining.

On the Road as a Chauffeur

When we hear the word *chauffeur*, we often think of someone driving shiny limousines with the rich and famous as passengers. But that is only part of the opportunities for chauffeurs. These road warriors may also drive vans and luxury vans, corporate sedans, and private cars. They may drive for limousine companies, government offices, private businesses, or individuals. Many chauffeurs drive large vans between hotels and airports, bus depots, or train stations. Some chauffeurs drive luxury cars or limousines to proms, weddings, and other social events; to conventions and business meetings; or to entertainment events such as movie premieres, theater show openings, and sporting events. Other chauffeurs provide full-time, personal service to the wealthy or to private companies. A few chauffeurs provide protective and antikidnap services. There is also a trend toward having chauffeurs work as full-service executive assistants, acting as drivers, secretaries, and itinerary planners.

Chauffeurs typically provide passengers with a high level of special service. They pay particular attention to opening doors, holding umbrellas when it is raining, and loading or unloading packages from the trunk of the vehicle. They may also deliver packages or pick up clients for their employers. Many chauffeurs provide amenities such as music, television, newspapers, magazines, and telephones that make riding in their limousines enjoyable.

Working Conditions

The needs of clients or an employer dictate the work hours of chauffeurs, so their hours can change from day to day. They must expect to spend considerable time waiting for their passengers. For example, they may pick newlyweds up and take them to the reception and then wait until the reception ends to take them to the airport. Or a personal chauffeur may take his employer to work, wait, drive the employer to a meeting, wait, return the employer to the office, wait, and then drive the employer home. Chauffeurs commonly work evenings and weekends and may be on call all day long. Chauffeurs who work for hotels, resorts, and companies typically have regular hours; however, they can expect to work shifts.

Like taxi drivers, chauffeurs transport a variety of people, from rock stars to high school students going to a prom, and must provide the appropriate level of service the passengers require. On the job, they usually are far more formally dressed than taxi drivers. Chauffeurs for businesspeople typically wear suits or even a uniform. Those who drive passengers to special events may even wear tuxedos. Chauffeurs driving shuttle vehicles may only need to wear neat and clean clothes.

Qualifications and Training

Many limousine companies have requirements for their drivers that exceed the standards and requirements put in place by local governments. These companies often have higher minimum age requirements and look for drivers with a high school diploma. They may also conduct an investigation into the driver's medical, credit, criminal, and driving records. In addition, companies look for drivers who are friendly and courteous and able to relate well to a wide variety of passengers.

In order to become a chauffeur, you will need to hold a regular driver's license and obtain a chauffeur's license by passing a written test or completing a chauffeur's training course. The test typically includes motor vehicle laws, safe driving practices, and regulations concerning chauffeuring. Some companies provide new drivers with on-the-job training, which may include learning to operate the vehicle's communication equipment and how to provide superior customer service. A company may require their drivers to complete reports after each driving job or at the end of their shifts.

Job Outlook and Earnings

Employment opportunities for chauffeurs will continue to grow, especially in metropolitan areas. Chauffeurs who work for limousine companies typically are paid by the hour and may have some benefits. They also receive tips. The amount depends on the level of service provided as well as the personal inclinations of the passenger. Drivers who work for businesses and individuals are usually salaried. Some chauffeurs own and operate their own vehicles and may work independently or offer their services to a variety of employers. Chauffeurs who work full-time can earn from $25,000 to $60,000 a year.

Driving for a Small Limousine Company

Kayla Love works as a chauffeur and limousine driver for a small limousine service. She has always enjoyed being on the road. When she saw a help wanted ad for a limousine driver, she couldn't resist trying to get the job. The company, A-1 Limousine Service, had been in business just one year when Kayla began working there. A-1 had six cars but has since grown to have more than twenty cars and SUVs. To begin with, Kayla worked part-time, which consisted of mostly weekend work. Many of her riders were people celebrating special events, such as weddings, birthdays, or graduations. Occasionally, Kayla would be called to pick up a customer at the airport or drive a business executive to a meeting or other event.

Kayla was soon offered a full-time position, which required her to be able to drive all types of vehicles owned by A-1. With some on-the-job training, she learned to drive each limousine, the Lincoln Town Cars, vans, and the stretch SUVs. The advantage of her new position allowed her to have many weekends off. Now most of her passengers are businesspeople or professionals.

Working with Passengers. When Kayla is driving businesspeople, she works hard at getting them to relax. She has noticed that people who fly into the airport are often stressed when they get into her car. Kayla tries to get them talking to help relieve some of the stress. However, she points out that it is important in this job to know when passengers want to talk and when they want to be left alone. One key signal for stopping any conversation efforts is seeing passengers take out their laptop computers. Meeting the client's needs ensures that Kayla will receive a good tip. Kayla frequently does airport runs as well as takes passengers to parties and concerts. Sometimes, the passengers will have extra tickets that they offer to her. When the company had a contract with a local radio station to chauffeur entertainers who were in the city to perform concerts, she received some backstage passes to the concerts. Her favorite was backstage passes to an Eagles farewell concert, since the Eagles is her favorite group.

The Financial Side of the Job. The chauffeurs at the limousine company are paid an hourly wage. Tips belong entirely to the driver and are not shared with the company. Kayla pays for her own uniform and cell phone, while the company supplies the car.

Kayla is able to get a lot of riders because she has been with the company for over five years. The owners usually call her first for extra trips because she is good with the customers. Some customers even request Kayla to be their driver. Drivers who are willing to work more hours or work late into the night—to 2 or 3 A.M.—can earn more.

Career Pluses and Minuses. Kayla likes working as a chauffeur because she is able to earn a good income while being on the move throughout her workday. She also likes to meet and talk to the people who come from all over the world.

Because she is a true road warrior, she likes the fact that she doesn't have to sit behind a desk every day. Kayla enjoys the freedom this job offers. No boss is looking over her shoulder. While she sometimes has to deal with difficult passengers, Kayla has learned ways to deal with them effectively and does not let them bother her. The requirement to drive in all kinds of weather can be a drawback to this job. Also, some customers don't tip or tip a very small amount.

Career Advice. Kayla urges those who are just starting out as chauffeurs to work hard and focus on customer service. It is very important to be prompt not only showing up for work, but also to be sure the customers get to their destinations on time. Beginning drivers shouldn't worry about the low income they are likely to earn at first. With experience, new drivers learn how to work with their passengers. Then the supervisors will notice their increasing expertise and begin to give them better job assignments, which will lead to better tips. Kayla's most important advice: look professional, talk like a professional, and be professional, and you will get professional rewards.

Driving a Hotel Shuttle Van

Salvador Bell drives a shuttle van for a hotel in Fort Wayne, Indiana. He also helps at the front desk and with the bellhop's duties between his driving runs. The shuttle he drives is a full-size van. Each seat is high backed and well padded for passenger comfort. Most of Salvador's runs are to the airport to pick up hotel guests who fly into the city for visits or business.

After graduating from high school in Mexico City, he came to the United States and began attending college and working. Salvador became interested in the hotel job because it offered the flexible hours he needed in order to attend an academy to become a certified travel agent and because it would give him valuable experience in the travel industry.

To be able to drive the hotel's shuttle van, Salvador had to earn his chauffeur's license. The local branch of the state's Bureau of Motor Vehicles gave Salvador the materials he needed to study in order to pass the written examination for the license. Salvador had to learn the rules of the road, regulations for chauffeurs, and special rules for drivers when they are transporting passengers. Salvador's license allows him to drive vehicles that carry fewer than fifteen passengers.

Salvador on the Road. Before Salvador goes out on the road, he performs a pretrip check of the shuttle. He checks the oil, tires, lights, and windshield wipers. He also checks to see that the shuttle is clean inside and out. Then, just before he pulls out, he checks his mirrors for proper alignment.

When hotel guests make reservations, they may ask to be picked up at the airport when they arrive. Other guests call from the airport and ask for shuttle service to the hotel. When Salvador travels to the airport to pick up or drop off guests, he must park in a designated location in order to avoid getting a parking ticket. If he is picking up passengers, he frequently has to look for them. This may require checking the flight monitors in the airport to see if a flight is delayed and, if so, for how long.

As soon as Salvador greets passengers, he helps them with their luggage and loads it into the van. Most of the people who ride in the shuttle are very interesting, friendly people. Salvador knows the importance of being courteous to the guests. One thing he really likes about this job is the opportunity to meet people from all over the world. Driving them around gives him the chance to learn about other countries.

Salvador's job is not limited to airport runs; he also transports people to other places throughout the city. In order to do this, he has become familiar with the city's streets, popular attractions, and local malls. Passengers frequently ask him which restaurants are good, what movies are playing, or what special events are taking place. Keeping up-to-date about what is going on in the city is essential for this shuttle van driver.

A Challenging Situation. Driving the hotel shuttle bus can sometimes be a challenge. Salvador often has passengers who have limited English skills. Communicating with them can be quite difficult. He remembers one incident in which a hotel guest from the Far East asked to be taken to a meeting at an industrial plant that was located well beyond the shuttle's twelve-mile travel limit. The guest couldn't understand why Salvador could not drive him to his meeting. The hotel management was finally able to help the guest understand and did get the guest a taxi so he could get to his meeting.

For More Information

To learn more about licensing requirements for employment as a taxi driver or chauffeur, contact the offices of local government agencies regulating taxicabs. To find out about job opportunities, contact local taxicab or limousine companies or state employment service offices. For the special firsthand knowledge of what is involved in a career driving a taxi, van, or limousine, talk to people who actually have these jobs.

If you want general information about the work of taxi drivers and the taxi industry, contact:

Taxicab, Limousine & Paratransit Association
3849 Farragut Avenue
Kensington, MD 20895
www.tlpa.org

Canadian Taxicab Association
251 Queen Street East
Toronto, ON M5A 1S6
Canada
www.cantaxi.ca

For general information about the work of limousine drivers, contact:

National Limousine Association
49 South Maple Avenue
Marlton, NJ 08053
www.limo.org

CHAPTER THREE

Driving Local Trucks

D
o you realize that the United States and Canadian economies could not function without truck drivers as there is so much freight to be transported? Just think about it: trucks move almost everything that you as a consumer purchase—from food to clothing to gasoline. As the saying goes, "If you bought it, a truck brought it." Although rail service can move freight long distances, only trucks can deliver it directly to most customers. Truckers drive two kinds of routes—local and long haul. They also typically drive different-sized vehicles. The local driver is most often behind the wheel of a much smaller vehicle than the tractor-trailers that long-haul drivers operate. Local trucks can even be delivery vans bringing flowers, cleaning services, and furniture to homes. Some local trucks, however, are tractor-trailers hauling building materials and groceries from warehouses to stores. Most local trucks weigh less than twenty-six thousand pounds.

Being a truck driver is a very popular occupation in both the United States and Canada. It is estimated that there are more than 3.3 million truck drivers in the United States and 260,000 in Canada. A majority of these drivers are operating local trucks. You see them on the streets in your cities and local highways. They are moving goods to factories, businesses, and all the places where you purchase food, clothing, gasoline, cars, lumber, furniture, appliances, and just about every product that you use in your daily life. Because of their ability to link up with ships, trains, and airplanes, local trucks usually make the initial pickup and final delivery of goods. Please remember that every time you see a truck in your community, there is a career opportunity for some driver, and that person on the move could possibly be you.

The History of Trucking

The word *truck* comes from the Greek word *trochos*, meaning "wheel." The earliest trucks were powered by steam and were only used to haul freight from factories to railroad stations. These trucks remained in use until the start of the First World War. The first gasoline-powered truck was built by Gottlieb Daimler of Germany in 1896. It had a four-horsepower engine and two speeds forward and one in reverse. Two years later, the Winton Company in the United States built a delivery truck with a single-cylinder, six-horsepower engine. These early trucks with their solid-rubber tires and primitive springs were driven over such poor roads that they gave the first truck drivers an incredibly rough ride. In fact, many of these trucks literally shook themselves apart. Nevertheless, they could move faster than the horse-drawn vehicles that had been used to carry goods. They weren't, however, able to carry very heavy loads. Often, the truck was heavier than the load it could carry. Nevertheless, in 1904, there were seven hundred trucks delivering goods locally in the United States. Longer hauls were done by boat or train. Today, there are in excess of fifteen million trucks in the United States and more than six hundred thousand registered trucks in Canada.

Trucks first showed how necessary they were when railroads were not able to move all the war supplies to the East Coast for shipment to Europe during the First World War. Convoys of trucks aided in this job. They had to follow very circuitous routes to find good roads and adequate bridges. This mass movement of goods was the beginning of intercity trucking.

Types of Trucks

As you have probably observed while driving down the road, trucks come in all sizes, from step-up vans to truck tractors drawing one or more trailers. By government regulation, trucks are typically classified by gross weight. Light trucks, which include vans and small pickups, weigh up to ten thousand pounds. Most trucks on the road fall into this category. Medium trucks weigh from ten thousand to twenty-six thousand pounds. These trucks usually have all axles attached to a single frame. Heavy trucks, such as tractor-trailers, weigh more than twenty-six thousand pounds. There are also specialty trucks such as tankers, garbage trucks, moving vans, lumber trucks, fire engines, concrete mixers, refrigerator trucks, and dry-bulk carriers. During their careers as truck drivers, most drivers operate more than one type of vehicle.

Career Opportunities in Truck Driving

When it comes to a career driving a truck, many options exist for you. You could work for a food, car, or furniture store that hauls only its own products or for a carrier that serves many shippers and receivers. In either case, the basic decision that you will have to make in this career is whether you wish to be a local (short-haul) driver or a long-haul driver, also known as an over-the-road driver. The major difference is that local truck drivers are assigned short runs that can usually be completed in a day, while long-haul drivers may be on the road for a week or more. Another difference is that local truck drivers operate all types of trucks, and long-haul drivers usually drive tractor-trailer trucks. In this chapter, the work of local truck drivers is explored in detail, while Chapter 4 describes the careers of long-haul drivers.

The Many Tasks of Local Truck Drivers

No matter what type of goods local drivers haul, they generally return to home base the same day. Some drivers never leave a city, while others may travel between several nearby cities. Drivers may have the same assignment every day, following a specific route. Others may make local deliveries or pickups that vary from day to day. And a few drivers may also have sales responsibilities. The work that individual drivers do depends on the products that they transport. For example, produce truckers usually pick up loaded trucks early in the morning and spend the rest of the day delivering produce to many different grocery stores. A lumber truck driver would make several trips from the lumberyard to one or more construction sites. Gasoline tank truck drivers pick up gas at a refinery and then deliver it to numerous gas stations in the course of a day.

A Typical Day for Most Local Truck Drivers

At the start of the workday, when local drivers leave the terminal or warehouse, they check their trucks for fuel and oil. They also inspect the trucks to make sure the brakes, windshield wipers, and lights are working and that a fire extinguisher, flares, and other safety equipment are aboard and in working condition. In addition, they have the responsibility of making sure the cargo is secure.

Typically, before the drivers arrive, material handlers have loaded the trucks and arranged the items in order of delivery to minimize handling of the goods. Drivers also need to adjust their mirrors so that both sides of the truck are visible from the driver's seat. Many companies require their drivers to follow a checklist to ensure that every safety step is followed. At the end of their inspection, drivers report to the dispatcher about equipment that does not work or is missing.

Before drivers begin their runs, they are given paperwork detailing their stops and what will be delivered and/or picked up at each stop. If they do not drive a regular route, the drivers choose the order of their stops and arrange the paperwork accordingly. At each stop, customers must sign receipts for the goods received or placed on the truck. If there is a cash-on-delivery (COD) arrangement, drivers must collect the balance due on the merchandise. Drivers try to deliver goods as fast as possible at each stop. This is often difficult because they may have to get in line behind other drivers who are also delivering goods. At the end of the workday, drivers return to the home base and turn in receipts, money, records of deliveries made, and any reports on mechanical problems with their trucks.

The Tasks of Driver/Sales Workers

Besides having all the responsibilities of local truck drivers, driver/sales workers perform many additional tasks at each stop and may use their selling abilities to increase sales and gain additional customers for their companies' products. This is a good job for drivers who want a greater variety of responsibilities.

Most of these drivers have wholesale routes delivering to businesses and stores rather than homes. You have probably seen some of these drivers in grocery stores arranging bread, cakes, rolls, and other baked goods on display racks. Bakery driver/sales workers also estimate the amount and variety of baked goods to stock by paying close attention to the items that sell well and those left sitting on the shelves. They may recommend changes in a store's order or may encourage the manager to stock new bakery products.

Drivers who service vending machines in factories, schools, and other buildings are another example of driver/sales workers. They check items remaining in the machines, replace stock, and remove money deposited in the cash boxes. They also examine each vending machine to make minor repairs, clean machines, and see that merchandise and change are being dispensed properly. After they have completed their routes, driver/sales workers order items for the next delivery based on what products have been selling well, the weather, the time of year, and any customer feedback.

Working Conditions for Local Truck Drivers

Every year, it becomes easier in many ways to be a truck driver. Trucks now ride more comfortably, paperwork is handled more efficiently, and traffic and weather reports are more accurate.

Nevertheless, driving a truck is physically demanding. Drivers are often required to unload goods at each stop. Some of this cargo, such as doors, mattresses, and office equipment, can be quite heavy. In fact, it may be so heavy that a helper rides with the driver to assist in lifting the cargo. Besides physical demands, driving a truck can be stressful. Traffic is very congested in many cities and on highways, and drivers may often just creep along in traffic with cars frequently cutting in front of them. When you are on the move all day in a truck, you quickly learn that not all drivers obey traffic laws. Plus, because it takes trucks so much longer to stop, you must anticipate what is going to happen next on the road far more than the driver of a passenger vehicle. In addition, you must endure hours of driving in the rain or on icy streets. Driving a truck requires concentration on the road at all times.

Days for local truck drivers can be long in order to complete all their deliveries. It is not unusual for drivers to work thirteen- to fifteen-hour days. Not all of these hours are spent behind the wheel, for state and federal laws usually limit this time to ten hours a day. The remainder of the time is typically spent waiting to get your truck loaded or unloaded. Driving a truck often involves working odd hours. Many local drivers begin their days as early as 2 A.M. This is especially true for those who handle food for chain grocery stores, produce markets, and bakeries. Because some cities have local ordinances that severely limit the number of hours that trucks can be on their streets during the day, local drivers may only be able to make deliveries at night.

In considering a career as a local truck driver, you need to be aware that your driving skills will be challenged daily, especially if you drive a tractor-trailer. You may need to maneuver down alleys where your clearance can be measured in inches, not feet. Plus, the most difficult thing for truck drivers to do is to back up. Unfortunately, local truck drivers have to do more backing up than any other truckers.

Qualifications and Training

State and provincial regulations govern the qualifications and standards for local truck drivers. However, drivers of hazardous materials and those who cross state or provincial lines must also comply with federal regulations. In addition to these regulations, many companies have their own standards that may be higher than state, provincial, or federal standards. You can also expect your employer to require a clean driving record.

Licensing. In the United States, all local truck drivers must have a state driver's license. A regular driver's license is often sufficient to drive light trucks and vans and will also enable you to drive within the borders of many states when you are only eighteen. If you will be driving a vehicle designed to carry at least twenty-six thousand pounds, which includes most tractor-trailers as well as bigger straight trucks, you will need a commercial driver's license (CDL) from the state in which you live. You will also need this license to operate trucks transporting hazardous materials and those engaged in interstate commerce no matter what the size of the truck.

To qualify for a commercial driver's license, you must be at least twenty-one years old and pass a written test on rules and regulations. Then you must demonstrate that you can actually operate a commercial truck safely in order to get this license. In addition, the state will check a national data bank to make sure that you have not had a license suspended or revoked in another state. The minimum requirements for this license are provided in Chapter 4, as long-haul drivers must also obtain commercial licenses. You can obtain information on how to apply for a commercial driver's license from your state's motor vehicle administration.

To drive a truck in Canada, regulations vary by province, but typically you need a special class license to drive a straight truck or articulating truck, such as a tractor-trailer. You may also need an air brake endorsement or a Transportation of Dangerous Goods (TDG) certification.

Training. Taking a driver training course in high school helps in preparing for a future career as a local truck driver, as is taking courses in automotive mechanics. You can also learn on the job, especially if you are driving a light truck or van. Companies prefer to train drivers of tractor-trailers in their own classes or for these drivers to have completed training programs with private or public vocational-technical schools. Carefully study the checklist for finding quality tractor-trailer driver training schools in Appendix A, as there are schools with courses that do not provide sufficient training or driving time to assure you a job on completion of their programs. You can also find industry-certified courses in schools through the website of the Professional Truck Driver Institute (www.ptdi.org/schools). Before enrolling in a school, you should also check with local trucking companies to make sure a school's training is acceptable.

Starting Out as a Truck Driver

As a new driver, you can expect to be assigned immediately to a regular driving job; however, some companies may start you out as a truck driver helper. When helpers gain experience and demonstrate their reliability, they receive driving assignments. It is also common to begin as an extra driver substituting for regular drivers who are ill or on vacation. Then, you will get a regular assignment when an opening occurs. New drivers sometimes start on panel or other small trucks and advance to larger and heavier trucks as they gain experience.

As a new driver, you can usually expect some informal training from your employer. It may consist of only a few hours of instruction from an experienced driver, sometimes on your own time. You may also ride with and observe experienced drivers before being assigned your own run. Some companies give one to two days of classroom instruction covering general duties, the operation and loading of a truck, company policies, and the preparation of delivery forms and company records. Plus, your first months as a driver may be made easier because you are assigned an experienced company driver as a mentor to answer your questions and give you advice. Driver/sales workers also receive training on the various company products so they will be more effective sales workers and better able to handle customer requests.

Job Outlook

There are thousands of local trucking companies all over the United States. Most of these firms primarily carry goods within a metropolitan area and nearby suburbs and nonurban areas. Not all of these companies offer job opportunities; many just have one driver who is also the owner. You are most likely to find a job with a small company because three out of four trucking companies employ fewer than ten drivers. Your opportunities are not limited to working for trucking companies; many businesses also hire local drivers. The good news is that truck driving has among the largest number of job openings of any occupation.

At the start of the twenty-first century, more than eighty thousand new local and long-haul truck drivers were needed each year, and a severe shortage of drivers to replace those who were leaving the field existed. How long truck drivers will be in such demand will depend on the strength of the economy. In good times, when the economy is strong, more freight is moved by trucks, and companies tend to hire more drivers. If the economy slows, companies hire fewer drivers or even lay off drivers. Overall, the employment of truck drivers through the year 2014 should grow, as the amount of freight carried by trucks is expected to increase. The increased use of rail, air, and ship transportation also requires more local drivers to pick up and deliver these shipments. Because truck driving does not require education beyond high school, you can expect to compete for those jobs that have the most attractive earnings and working conditions.

Canadians can expect similar growth in the trucking industry, with an average employment growth rate projected for all types of truck drivers.

The one area in which the demand for truck drivers will grow slowly is in driver/sales worker jobs. This is because companies are increasingly splitting their responsibilities among other workers. Sales, ordering, and customer service tasks are being shifted to sales and office staffs, and regular truck drivers are being used to make deliveries to customers.

Earnings

Local truck driving jobs vary greatly in terms of earnings, weekly work hours, and the quality of equipment operated. As you gain experience in this career, you will become a more valued worker and enjoy increased earnings. Also, the size and type of truck that you drive affects your pay, with those driving larger trucks earning more money. Employers pay local truck drivers an hourly rate and extra pay for working overtime, usually after forty hours. Benefits, including health insurance and sick and vacation leave, are common in the trucking industry. Plus, performance-related bonuses are given, especially for those with safe driving records. Truck drivers earn on average between $12.67 and $20.09 per hour, with top wage earners getting over $24.00 per hour. Canadian truck drivers earn between C$10.70 and C$14.06 with top pay being about C$20.00 per hour. About 21 percent of all truckers are union members, with most belonging to the International Brotherhood of Teamsters.

On the Job with a Local Truck Driver

Brent Lindke is an experienced local truck driver. This is an excellent career choice for him, as he has always loved to drive and doesn't want to be in an office all day. Besides, this career choice has allowed him to achieve his childhood dream of driving a big truck. Before taking his present job with a company that distributes wood products to building supply companies such as Home Depot, Brent worked in the industry as a long-haul driver. He firmly believes that he was hired for his current job because he had so much driving experience.

Brent currently drives a tractor-trailer that is so new, he hasn't had time yet to install his CB radio. The cab has two seats, but only his seat is an air-ride seat that takes much of the bounce out of driving on uneven roads. Although the panel appears to have a great number of gauges to study, the only additions beyond what a car might have are air gauges that tell him if he has sufficient air for braking. As he drives along, Brent frequently checks the air, water, and oil gauges to make sure that he catches a potential problem before it can occur. He also watches the speedometer because drivers can lose their jobs and licenses if they have too many speeding tickets. His rig is equipped with an engine governor that will not let him go over sixty-eight miles per hour.

Brent always concentrates intently on what is happening on the road. While the drivers of passenger cars typically observe only several cars in front of them, he must observe at least a distance of two blocks because it takes him so much longer than a car to stop. Brent, however, does not just look forward; he must also use the side mirrors to locate the cars beside and behind his truck. This is not totally successful because trucks have significant blind spots where drivers simply cannot see cars no matter how many mirrors they have.

On the Road with Brent. The job of driving a tractor-trailer in one of the most congested traffic areas in Northern California is not an easy task. Also, being a local driver may involve more organization, paperwork, lifting, and long days than you ever imagined. Each week, Brent usually works four very long days of thirteen to fifteen hours; however, by law he can only drive for ten of those hours in a day. In a typical day, he makes from ten to eighteen stops on a route that goes from Sacramento to as far south as San Jose and back to Sacramento. This usually involves driving from 300 to 360 miles, although it could be as many as 500 miles.

On workdays, Brent gets up at 2:15 A.M. so he can be at the terminal by 3 A.M. Although the truck is already loaded, he must make sure that the load is properly strapped down. He also has to check the truck from bumper to bumper to make sure that it is safe to be on the road. And he studies the papers detailing where he will stop, what will be delivered at each stop, and the location of the products on the truck. By 3:45 A.M., Brent is usually ready to pull out of the terminal to begin his route.

The First Delivery. Brent drives through San Francisco on a freeway to arrive at his first stop at a twenty-four-hour Home Depot store at 5:45 A.M. As usual, there are many other trucks in front of him, and he has to wait his turn. He immediately checks in and finds out where he should park. Most days, he has to wait from thirty minutes to an hour to get unloaded at this busy store. Brent uses this time to update his logbook, which is a record of what he is doing every fifteen minutes throughout the workday. He also chats with other drivers and perhaps eats something for breakfast. During the waiting time, Brent continually inches the truck forward until it is time for it to be unloaded. Then, he puts on work gloves and pulls back the truck's side curtains so the forklift driver can easily remove a pallet of cedar closet liners. As soon as the appropriate paperwork is signed, Brent begins to maneuver away from the docking area. The entire delivery has taken forty-five minutes. To leave, he has to make a sharp left turn around the building and avoid hitting piles of products that are stacked along his path. Some backing up is required to make the turn.

The Second Delivery. Brent only has to travel across a parking lot to reach his second delivery site. Since so many trucks are ahead of his, he decides to unload the products himself in order to arrive early for his next delivery. This requires him to get a lumber cart and lift four heavy doors (seventy-five to one hundred pounds each) from the truck and place them on the cart. It takes him about ten minutes to unload the products and another ten minutes for the company representative to check that the product is not damaged and to complete the paperwork.

The Remainder of the Day. Throughout the day, while Brent waits for his truck to be unloaded, he updates his log, studies the paperwork for the remaining deliveries, and eats the food he has brought with him.

Brent's workday began at 3 A.M. By 8:15, he has made three deliveries. He needs to make ten more before he can return home. He faces heavy traffic until about 10 A.M., then it will be lighter, except for the noon hour and commuter rush periods. Brent will probably not be back at the supply terminal until about 6:30 P.M., and he will have spent more than fifteen hours on the job during this typical day.

Career Advice. Brent admits that being a local truck driver is not the right career for everyone. Although he loves being a road warrior and being able to be home each evening, the major downside of this job for him is having to get up so early four days a week. He advises anyone considering a career in this field to find a local driver and ride with him or her for a day or more to see exactly what this career is like. And if you are still in school, he believes that you should pay close attention to mathematics, physics, and geography, as you will use these subjects every day as a truck driver.

Another Route to Being a Local Truck Driver

Brent Lindke learned how to drive trucks by going to a driving school. This is not the route that Kurt Zimmerman followed in first becoming a local driver and then a long-haul driver. He learned to drive on the job. After completing high school and some college, Kurt worked in sales. One day, he saw a line outside the trucking firm next door to his office. Because he was curious, he discovered that the company was looking for workers and offering a very good wage. Kurt decided to interview and was hired on the spot for a job as a fueler at a trucking terminal. Company personnel informally taught Kurt, and soon he was driving trucks to and from the fueling station. He admits that he ground a lot of gears while learning to drive. Kurt also discovered that he really liked the idea of becoming a driver and obtained a license. Because he displayed initiative, the trucking company put him on the road with the safety director, and he learned by trial and error to drive a truck with a forty-eight-foot trailer.

Kurt's Job as a Local Truck Driver. One day while Kurt was working as a fueler, the trucking company had a load that needed to be driven immediately to Rockford, Illinois, from the Chicago area where he worked. The dispatcher asked Kurt to handle this assignment even though Kurt explained that he was not a very experienced driver and had never been to Rockford. The dispatcher said this was the way for him to learn, so Kurt soon found himself on the road following a map and making his first delivery. The entire round-trip was a hundred miles.

Because Kurt completed this first trip successfully, the company soon asked him to become a driver doing local jobs within one hundred miles of the terminal. He delivered all kinds of products to homes, hospitals, and businesses. Besides driving, Kurt helped load and unload the cargo, which required a strong back. Occasionally, he needed a helper because the loads were so heavy. He especially remembers having to lift cases of books up several flights of stairs. His job also involved doing a lot of map reading to find delivery places. Often, he would need to contact the local police to find out what route he should take because trucks are prohibited on many city streets. Sometimes, he even needed to obtain a permit to drive on side streets.

For more than thirteen years, Kurt was a local truck driver. During this time, he had several memorable experiences, as all drivers do. One time, he was delivering more than fifty thousand baby chickens to a research facility. Unfortunately, several of the boxes came open, and six hundred chickens were suddenly loose in the truck. It was not easy for him to get so many chickens back in their boxes. Kurt also remembers opening the door of a truck he was unloading and coming face-to-face with a rattlesnake that had hitched a ride from Texas.

During his years as a local trucker, Kurt especially enjoyed having such close contact with the people receiving the products that he delivered. He left this position to become a long-haul driver because, as a true road warrior, he wanted to see more places.

Driving a Truck for a Produce Company

Don Benson is a local truck driver who delivers produce for the Piazza Produce Company of Indianapolis. He drives an eighteen-foot, low-profile truck with a refrigerated box. His route takes him to several cities and small towns in Northeast Indiana. Don's day begins at 4 A.M., when he gets to the produce company where he performs a pretrip check of his truck, including lights, tires, and flashers. The produce has already been loaded into the truck by the overnight crew. Once Don has picked up the invoices for the day's deliveries, it is time for this road warrior to begin his route.

At each delivery point, Don must unload the produce listed on that customer's invoice. Using a two-wheeled hand truck, he takes the orders into schools, restaurants, and businesses. At some stops, he must rotate the stock on the shelves. At others, he only has to place the produce in the designated receiving area so that the employees can then store it properly. When his route is complete, Don returns to the terminal and does a post-trip check of the truck. If there are any mechanical problems, he must fill out a form requesting repairs.

Career Pluses and Minuses. Don learned about his job from his brother, who worked for the company. He knew that he would like this job because he would get to be outside throughout the day. Now that he is on the job, Don really likes driving his truck, seeing the scenery along the route, and meeting lots of people along the way. He feels a great sense of freedom and relaxation as he drives his route and delivers produce. Don also likes being fully responsible for making his deliveries as quickly and efficiently as possible. In this job, he is his own boss when he is out on his route.

Don's route requires him to travel about 315 miles every day. Accidents and bad weather can really slow him down, keeping him on the road as late as 7 P.M. and forcing him to work a fifteen-hour day. As Don travels along his route on interstate highways and city streets, he is very aware of the other drivers on the road who don't want to get stuck behind his truck. It is not unusual for him to be cut off by drivers who are in a hurry and make risky maneuvers. These drivers frustrate Don because he feels that he must second-guess them in order to avoid accidents. He also has to be very cautious in the heavy traffic he often encounters on narrow city streets.

Driving for a Local Company

Most of the drivers that have been described in this chapter work for trucking companies. There are also many job opportunities to drive for other companies picking up and delivering goods. Some of these jobs require you to drive a tractor-trailer, while others involve driving smaller trucks, vans, and pickups. Here is a list of the types of companies where you might find a job as a local truck driver.

appliance stores
beverage companies
building supply companies
cleaners
commercial bakeries
construction companies
department stores
flower shops
furniture stores
gasoline companies

grocery suppliers
hardware stores
local movers
lumberyards
milk companies
nurseries
office supply companies
plumbing companies
tire companies
waste removal companies

For More Information

You can find out more about job opportunities for local truck drivers from local trucking companies and local offices of the state employment service.

More information on career opportunities in truck driving may be obtained from:

American Trucking Associations
950 North Glebe Road, Suite 210
Arlington, VA 22203
www.truckline.com

Canadian Trucking Alliance
324 Somerset Street West
Ottawa, ON K2P 0J9
Canada
www.cantruck.com

The Professional Truck Driver Institute, a nonprofit organization established by the trucking industry, manufacturers, and others, certifies truck driver training programs meeting industry standards. A free list of certified tractor-trailer driver training programs and a booklet, *Careers in Trucking*, may be obtained from:

Professional Truck Driver Institute
555 East Braddock Road
Alexandria, VA 22314
www.ptdi.org

Information for truck driver training in Canada can be obtained from:

Truck Training Schools Association of Ontario
www.ttsao.com

Information on union truck driving, labor studies, and training as well as useful links to other websites can be obtained from:

International Brotherhood of Teamsters
25 Louisiana Avenue NW
Washington, DC 20001
www.teamsters.org

Teamsters Canada
#804-2540 Daniel-Johnson
Laval, QC H7T 2S3
Canada
www.teamsters.ca

CHAPTER FOUR

Driving Long-Haul Trucks

D rive along any major highway in the United States or Canada, and you will notice huge trucks and tractor-trailers from different states and provinces. They will be hauling automobiles, petroleum products, food, bulk goods, chemicals, building materials, furniture, electronics gear, and just about everything imaginable that needs to be moved from one area of each country to another or between the two nations. The drivers of most of these trucks are long-haul truckers. Their job is quite different from that of local truck drivers who work close to their homes. On one trip, a long-haul driver could drive from the West Coast to the East Coast, continue up into Canada, and stop in the Midwest on the way down to Texas before returning home. If you buy furniture from North Carolina, it will be a long-haul truck driver who transports it to your home in New Mexico. If you eat an orange in Minneapolis or Toronto, it was probably brought there from Florida, California, or Texas by a long-haul trucker. These drivers also transport new cars from Detroit to Iowa, seafood from Newfoundland to New York City, and computers from Silicon Valley to Atlanta and Ottawa. They bring products from manufacturers to retailers and raw materials to processing plants.

Before the development of the interstate system in the United States in the mid-1950s and the federal-provincial system in Canada at about the same time, most goods were moved across these countries by rail. This is no longer true. Trucks have now totally eclipsed the railroads as cross-country carriers of most goods. Being a long-haul truck driver will not only keep you on the move, it also keeps commerce in North America moving.

A Look at Trucking Companies

There is no shortage of companies offering truck drivers jobs that allow them to drive long distances, since there are more than thirty-nine thousand companies in the United States and more than two thousand companies in Canada. As a long-haul driver on the move, you can work for a company that delivers freight across the country or a regional firm that makes deliveries in several states or provinces. The companies range in size from giants like Schneider National Carriers and Yellow Freight Systems with thousands of drivers to small companies with only one or two drivers. You will also have the opportunity to work for a company that hauls its own products, such as Wal-Mart or Kroger.

Long-distance trucking companies transport a wide variety of goods in numerous types of vehicles, from refrigerated trailers to tankers to flatbeds. These companies operate as both truckload (TL) or less-than-truckload (LTL) carriers. The truckload carriers move large amounts of goods directly to their destinations, usually with no stops in between. They carry full single loads that are not combined with other shipments. LTL carriers pick up multiple shipments and take them to a terminal, where they are unloaded and then reloaded by destination. Then the shipments are carried to distant terminals near their destinations. Local truck drivers complete the delivery chain.

The trucking company where you choose to work may also offer a wide variety of services designed to improve the efficient transfer of goods. For example, with "just-in-time" shipping, trucking companies deliver goods from suppliers just in time for their use. For a driver, this creates the responsibility of meeting tight schedules without fail.

Driving Long-Haul Trucks

Long-haul truck driving is a full-time job that takes many drivers across the country and even into adjoining countries. When you aren't driving, you may spend your time in a small compartment attached to the cab. These compartments range in size from being a simple bunk to a mini-apartment on wheels with closets, storage space, and sleeping and cooking facilities. Plus, they are likely to have a TV. If you are like most drivers, you will occasionally spend a night in a motel room for its comfort. You will typically bathe at truck stops.

In the past, being a long-haul driver was a very solitary life, except for talking to other drivers as you traveled and at truck stops. This is no longer true. More and more companies are using two drivers on very long runs—one drives while the other sleeps in a berth behind the cab. These drivers are often husband and wife teams. "Sleeper" runs may last for days or even weeks, usually with the truck stopping only for fuel, food, loading, and unloading. On some trips, considerable time may be spent waiting to have the truck loaded or unloaded.

While some long-distance drivers have regular runs transporting freight to the same city, others perform unscheduled runs and may have no idea of where they will go on a run. For example, a driver may set out from Chicago carrying books to Ohio. From there, the dispatcher may send the driver to Miami with tires. Before a run ends, the driver may also go to Dallas, Phoenix, cross into Mexico, then on to Los Angeles, Seattle, over the border to British Columbia, and down to Omaha before returning to Chicago.

The Tasks of Long-Haul Truck Drivers

Long-haul drivers can expect to spend most of their working hours behind the wheel; however, they may load or unload their cargo after arriving at a destination. This is especially true if you decide to haul specialty cargo because you are likely to be the only one at the destination familiar with the procedure or certified to handle it. As an auto-transport driver, for example, you would be expected to drive and position cars on the trailers and head ramps and remove them at the dealerships.

The Professional Truck Driver Institute lists the following duties as the primary functions of long-haul truck drivers:

1. Read and interpret control systems
2. Perform vehicle inspections
3. Exercise basic control
4. Execute shifting
5. Back and dock tractor-trailer
6. Couple trailer
7. Uncouple trailer
8. Perform visual search
9. Manage and adjust vehicle speed
10. Manage and adjust vehicle space relations
11. Check and maintain vehicle systems and components
12. Diagnose and report malfunctions
13. Identify potential driving hazards and perform emergency maneuvers
14. Identify and adjust to difficult and extreme driving conditions
15. Handle and document cargo
16. Act responsibly with accident scenes and reporting procedures
17. Be aware of and responsible for environmental issues
18. Plan trips and make appropriate decisions
19. Use effective communication and public relations skills
20. Manage personal resources and cope with life on the road
21. Record and maintain hours of service requirement

Working Conditions

Today, long-distance truck driving has become far less physically demanding because most of these trucks now have comfortable seats, good ventilation, and improved, ergonomically designed cabs. Nevertheless, driving for many hours at a stretch and loading and unloading cargo can be tiring. Plus, there is the mental strain of navigating such a large vehicle through traffic and into tight docking areas, as well as the challenge of coping with variable weather and traffic conditions. For example, all in one day, a driver may experience driving in an unusual spring snowstorm in the mountains and on crowded city streets. Long-haul truckers also face boredom, loneliness, and fatigue and may only return to their homes once a month. Some self-employed long-haul truck drivers who own and operate their trucks spend most of the year away from home. Nevertheless, most drivers enjoy the independence and lack of supervision found in long-distance driving.

As a long-haul driver, expect to frequently travel at night, on holidays, and on weekends to avoid traffic delays and to deliver cargo on time. How long you drive each day and week in the United States is regulated by the Department of Transportation. You may drive for eleven hours and work for up to fourteen hours—including driving and nondriving duties—after having ten hours off duty. You will not be able to drive after having worked for sixty hours in the past seven days or seventy hours in the past eight days unless you have taken at least thirty-four consecutive hours off duty. Canada, has federally regulated fourteen-day cycles, with specific driving and rest period limitations.

If you are like most drivers on long runs, you will work close to the maximum time permitted because what you earn is typically based on the number of miles or hours you drive. Plus, you will usually be required to document your time in a logbook.

Design improvements in newer trucks and technological advances are doing much to reduce the stress of long-distance driving. Satellites and global positioning systems (GPS) link many of these state-of-the-art vehicles with company headquarters. Today, troubleshooting, directions, weather reports, and other important communications can be delivered to trucks anywhere they are located within seconds. Furthermore, drivers can easily communicate with dispatchers to discuss delivery schedules and courses of action in the event of mechanical problems. The satellite linkup also allows dispatchers to track a truck's location, fuel consumption, and engine performance. Some drivers also work with computerized inventory-tracking equipment that allows the producer, warehouse, and customer to know the product's location at all times.

Job Qualifications

Qualifications for a job as a long-haul truck driver in the United States are far more demanding than those for local drivers. You must meet the following minimum requirements prescribed in the Federal Motor Carrier Safety Regulations.

- **Age:** Drivers must be at least twenty-one years of age to drive trucks across state lines.
- **License:** All drivers must obtain a commercial driver's license (CDL) issued by the state in which they live. To qualify for a CDL, you must pass a written test on rules and regulations, then demonstrate that you can operate a commercial truck safely. Contact your state Department of Motor Vehicles for more information about this license.
- **Training:** Entry-level drivers must complete the training required by the Federal Motor Carrier Safety Administration.
- **Physical Requirements:** Drivers will need to pass a physical examination once every two years. The main physical requirements include good hearing, twenty-forty vision with or without corrective lenses, and a seventy-degree field

of vision in each eye. Drivers cannot be color-blind and must be able to hear a forced whisper in one ear at not less than five feet with or without a hearing aid. Drivers must have normal use of arms and legs and normal blood pressure. You will not be able to be an interstate truck driver if you have epilepsy or diabetes controlled by insulin.

- **Driving Record:** Drivers may not have been convicted of a felony involving the use of a motor vehicle, driving under the influence of drugs or alcohol, or hit-and-run driving that resulted in injury or death.
- **Education:** All drivers must be able to read and speak English well enough to read road signs, prepare reports, and communicate with law enforcement officers and the public.
- **Safety:** Drivers must learn and comply with the safety rules of the U.S. Department of Transportation and take a written test on the department's Motor Carrier Safety Regulations.
- **Substance Abuse:** Federal regulations require employers to test drivers for alcohol and drug use as a condition of employment and require periodic random tests while on duty. Drivers must have no convictions for drug-related crimes.

Besides complying with federal regulations, U.S. drivers must also meet state regulations that can be in excess of those requirements. Also, you will find that many trucking companies have even higher standards than those listed in this book. Many firms require drivers to be at least twenty-two years old, be able to lift heavy objects, and have driven trucks for three to five years. Plus, companies often prefer to hire high school graduates and may require annual physical examinations.

In Canada, the federal government does not play as active a role in regulating the qualifications and standards for drivers. Most of these regulations are made by the individual provincial governments and are similar to regulations in the United States.

Training

Very few jobs entail so much personal responsibility as being the driver of a long-distance truck. While drivers can now get advice more easily from dispatchers, customers, other truck drivers, and highway patrol officers, in the end it is the drivers who have their hands on the wheels. They have the difficult task of bringing a more than $100,000 vehicle with all its cargo to a receiver on time, undamaged, and safely. This requires training.

Some states and provinces require prospective drivers to complete a training course in basic truck driving before being issued a license to drive a long-haul truck. The Professional Truck Driver Institute (PTDI), a nonprofit organization established by the trucking industry, manufacturers, and others, certifies driver training courses at truck driver training schools that meet industry standards as well as Federal Highway Administration and provincial guidelines for training tractor-trailer drivers. You can find schools offering entry-level courses at www.ptdi.org/schools. You should also review the checklist for finding quality tractor-trailer driver training courses in Appendix A.

Attending a training school is not the only way to learn how to become a long-haul truck driver. Some drivers have been trained in the military. Large trucking companies also may have their own formal training programs that prospective drivers attend. Other companies assign experienced drivers to teach and mentor newer drivers.

Going into Business for Yourself

While the overwhelming majority of all long-distance drivers work for a trucking company or a firm hauling its own products, some purchase a truck and go into business for themselves. Although many of these owner-operators are successful and earn more than truckers who work for others, some fail to cover expenses and eventually go out of business. To succeed as an owner-operator, you need a good business sense as well as truck driving experience. Taking courses in accounting, business, and business mathematics is helpful. Plus, knowledge of truck mechanics can help owner-operators save money by being able to perform their own routine maintenance and minor repairs.

Job Outlook and Earnings

There is a shortage of skilled long-haul drivers in both the United States and Canada. Both trucking companies and companies operating their own fleets in the two countries are having a difficult time finding the drivers that they need. Many are even offering bonuses to new drivers. In fact, there is almost no limit to the hiring needs of trucking companies. In Canada, positions are being opened up to residents of other countries. Some companies in the United States are experiencing as high as 100 percent turnover in a year. In Canada, the industrywide turnover rate for larger for-hire motor carriers is about 35 percent. Although truck driving pays relatively well, many people leave the career because of the lengthy periods away from home, long hours of driving, and the negative public image drivers face. The American Trucking Associations project a shortage of 110,000 drivers by 2014, a gap attributed partly to retirements and inadequate recruitment, plus increased demand for trucking.

Long-haul truck drivers typically earn more than local drivers. Most are paid by the mile. The rate per mile can vary greatly from employer to employer and may even increase with the type of cargo. For example, drivers of trucks carrying flammable materials are paid higher rates than other drivers. A few drivers work on commission. These drivers earn a fixed percentage of the profits that their employers make on each trip.

Typically, earnings increase with mileage driven, seniority, and the size and type of truck. Those drivers with the most seniority earn the most because they get the best assignments. The median annual salary of long-haul truck drivers is more than $40,000 in most areas of the United States. Those earning the highest income are the drivers who are self-employed with a median annual income close to $60,000. In Canada, drivers who work for a trucking company enjoy a median annual income of about C$40,000.

America's Road Team Captains

America's Road Team captains are exceptional professional truck drivers who have excellent safety records and outstanding communication skills. The team is sponsored by the American Trucking Associations and Volvo Trucks North America and has the responsibility of representing the more than five million professional truck drivers employed in this country. Within the industry, America's Road Team captains meet with fellow drivers, truck driver trainees, and safety managers. They appear at truck shows and truck stops and participate in truck driving championships, motor carrier safety banquets, driver awards programs, driver education classes, and high school career days. In addition, they speak to a variety of groups answering questions about what the trucking industry is doing to improve highway safety and reduce accidents as well as providing safe-driving tips and offering advice for sharing the road with large trucks. America's Road Team captains serve twenty-four months as captains and then continue reaching out to the public and industry on a smaller scale.

A Truck Driving Champion

America's Road Team captain Dennis Day is a true road warrior with tremendous enthusiasm for his career as a long-haul driver. From the time he was eight years old, he was fascinated by trucks. On his way home from school, he would stop at the library and check out books on trucks and devour them from cover to cover. At age eleven, Dennis secured a job cleaning a lot where truckers stopped. The drivers would let him clean the lights on their trucks and climb in the cab. Although he was very young, Dennis immediately decided that trucking was the life for him, and after twenty years of driving a truck, he still feels the same way. At fifteen, his interest in trucks gained another boost from his job at a warehouse loading and unloading trucks. To his delight, he got to know the drivers and listen to their stories about life on the road. Dennis stayed with this company until he was twenty-one and could begin his career as a trucker by going to driving school.

Throughout his career, Dennis has received recognition for his truck driving skills. He has won the Georgia State Truck Driving Championship eight times and been a runner-up in the national championships. These contests measure the skills of drivers. They involve a skill test, a written test, an interview, and the driver's ability to find defects on a truck that were placed there by the test givers. Dennis has driven more than two million accident-free miles.

A Look at Dennis's Workplaces. When Dennis was ready to become a truck driver, it was hard to get a job. The company where he trained required him to buy a tractor before he could take its course. Once he completed the course, the company supplied him with loads and soon he was driving all over the country by himself—living his boyhood dream. He would stay out on the road for three weeks at a time—the farther he traveled, the better. He remained with this company for two and a half years.

For his second job, Dennis chose to work for a company hauling telephone supplies from its distribution center in Norcross, Georgia, to the company's supply centers all over the country. Sometimes, he would drop a trailer and pick up a loaded one to bring back. Other times, he would have to unload the trailer and bring back return goods. In this job, he would leave Sunday night and be back on Thursday night or Friday morning. To him, it was almost like driving a local route. Dennis had planned to stay with this company; however, a change in management led to the elimination of the company's trucking department. He then went to Con-way Freight and remains with this company today. The company is a market leader in the supply chain management industry. Its services are used by some four hundred thousand customers throughout the world.

On the Job. Dennis loves the importance of his job as he is ensuring that key businesses in two southeastern cities have the supplies that they need within twenty-four hours. During the day, city drivers pick up shipments throughout the Atlanta area and bring them to the Con-way terminal in Lawrenceville—thirty-five miles northeast of Atlanta. The shipments are then put into trailers destined for other Con-way terminals. Dennis drives from the Atlanta terminal to the company's Tallahassee terminal pulling two twenty-eight-foot trailers behind his tractor five times a week. He leaves at nine or ten o'clock at night and is on the road for five hours with at least one or possibly two breaks for coffee and to stretch his legs. He leaves his trailers at the terminal in Tallahassee; however, he has to use forklifts to load two other trailers for the return trip to Atlanta. When the trailers are filled, Dennis departs and typically arrives back in Atlanta around ten in the morning. He makes five runs a week and drives twenty-nine hundred miles.

Dennis likes night driving, as many truckers do, because there is less traffic. Plus, he says that there is another world out there at night. During his trips, he talks to other drivers on his CB radio and monitors channel 19 for accidents. Dennis also listens to satellite radio for instant weather and traffic information.

Two Veteran America's Road Team Drivers

Marty and Lisa Fortun have received many industry awards for safety and their driving skills. As veteran members of the Road Team, they speak to students on high school career days. Besides explaining what it is like to be a truck driver, they point out the importance of studying math, foreign language, and geography in preparation for this career. They tell the students how they use math in determining when and where they will stop for fuel and how the load should be distributed correctly. They explain how helpful studying a foreign language is in order to be prepared to drive in another country. And they spell out how helpful it is to know geography in order to anticipate what the terrain will be like along the trip route.

A Family Tradition of Trucking. Marty's dad, younger brother, and many aunts and uncles are all truck drivers. In fact, his first job as a long-haul driver was on a team with his father. Lisa's parents were a driving team, just as she and Marty are today. Together, they drive a dedicated route, which involves following the same schedule each week. Every Sunday, they pull out of Green Bay, Wisconsin, pulling two trailers full of truck parts for two company terminals. They leave one in Seville, Ohio, and the other in Carlisle, Pennsylvania. At each terminal, they pick up a trailer already loaded with truck parts that can be repaired and return to Green Bay on Monday. They only stay in Green Bay long enough to pick up trailers to drive to Indianapolis, Indiana, and Charlotte, North Carolina, before returning to Green Bay on Wednesday.

Except for a six- to seven-hour layover that allows them to go home on Wednesday, they drive around the clock. Their final trip of the week is to Gary, Indiana, and West Memphis, Arkansas, which allows them to return to Green Bay very early Friday morning. They then start this route all over again on Sunday morning. In recent years, the possibility of driving dedicated routes has increased, allowing drivers like Marty and Lisa to have more time at home. Because they love being on the move together, they think team driving is a great career.

Combining Long-Haul Driving and Another Career

For ten months of the year, Roger Harrington has two careers. He is both a long-haul driver and a mechanic on a drag-racing team. As a driver of one of the team's two eighteen-wheelers, he transports racing cars, car parts, tires, tools, oil, fuel, uniforms, and everything else it takes to operate on the road. During racing season, he is gone from the team's headquarters in Indianapolis for one to six weeks, depending on the racing schedule. When the team leaves Indianapolis for a race, each truck has two drivers so they can drive straight through to the racetrack.

Once the team arrives at the track, Roger works as one of the eight mechanics programming the cars for the race. Then during the race, he and the other mechanics act as the pit crew. Typically, the qualifying runs are held on Friday and Saturday, and the four runs to the finals are on Sunday. After each race, the team returns to Indianapolis the next day, unless another race is scheduled for the following weekend. In that case, they usually go on to the next racetrack.

Roger worked on the team as a mechanic before he became one of its drivers. When the team needed another long-haul driver, he obtained a learner's permit and was taught how to drive by one of the team's experienced drivers. Not only did Roger see learning to drive a truck as a way to help the team, he also believed that it might lead to other career opportunities. His two careers have let him travel around the country and enjoy the tremendous exhilaration of seeing a car that he has worked on do well.

For More Information

Begin by checking out the resources listed at the end of Chapter 3. These organizations can give you more information on career opportunities in long-haul trucking. To learn what the life of a long-haul truck driver is really like, it is very helpful to talk to someone who is actually engaged in this occupation.

Trucking companies vary in size from those with thousands of vehicles to those with only one truck. To learn more about what employment opportunities actually exist, visit the websites of several trucking companies as well as several online employment sites. Appendix B provides a list of the names and addresses of the largest truck carriers by fleet size.

Because many long-haul drivers are members of the International Brotherhood of Teamsters, you may wish to find out more information about being a union worker by visiting the organization's website at www.teamsters.org (www.teamsters.ca in Canada). The websites also have useful links to other sites related to truck driving.

CHAPTER FIVE

Driving Buses

f you were going to drive an omnibus, do you know what you would be driving? *Omnibus* is a Latin word meaning "for all." It was eventually abbreviated to the word *bus*. As you know, a bus is a vehicle that typically transports passengers on designated routes. Some seat as few as eight passengers, and others can carry more than one hundred. When you drive a bus, not only are you on the move in your job, you are also providing an important service by helping to reduce the number of cars on the highway, thereby reducing consumption of gas as well as lessening some air pollution. Plus, buses let the people riding on them do things that they shouldn't do when driving their own cars. They can read a book, use their laptops, talk on cell phones, or listen to music.

Millions of North Americans depend on buses to get safely to their jobs, schools, and other destinations. In fact, buses transport far more people than airlines or railroads. Buses are also the safest way to travel on streets, roads, and highways because they are involved in far fewer accidents than passenger cars, trucks, and motorcycles.

Imagine sitting behind the wheel of a forty-five-foot bus traveling down a narrow street in heavy, rush-hour traffic toward the next stop. There are twenty-five or thirty passengers behind you talking loudly, and someone is asking you where the next stop is. It is beginning to rain, and a car has just turned in front of you. Can you handle this demanding situation? If so, then driving a bus may be a good career choice for you.

If you elect to become a bus driver, four basic jobs are available. You can become a school bus driver transporting students to and from school and school-related activities, a local transit bus driver carrying people within a city, an intercity bus driver transporting people from city to city within a state or province or across a country, or a motor coach driver taking passengers on tours or charter excursions. No matter which job you choose, you will be on the move behind the wheel almost every minute of your workday, whether you are driving a small ten-passenger vehicle, a very long city bus, or a forty-five-foot luxury motor coach.

A Look at Buses over Time

The first bus was probably a stagecoach driven by a steam engine in about 1830. Of course, it had no resemblance to a modern bus. Nor did the early buses in the United States, which were really cars lengthened to hold more passengers. By the 1920s, buses were mounted on a truck chassis, as modern school buses still are.

Today, you have the choice of driving several different types of buses. School buses carry fifty children and have special lights and safety features. Local transit buses seat about eighty passengers and have a low-ride platform, two entrances, low-back seats, and no space for luggage. Intercity and motor coach buses have high-back seats, luggage compartments and racks, reading lights, a restroom, and only one entrance. They typically carry about forty-seven passengers.

Working Conditions

Bus drivers have a challenging task in coping with passengers and traffic. This job can be stressful and fatiguing. On the positive side, many drivers like working independently, knowing that everything happening on the bus is their responsibility. They are the captains, and the buses are their ships.

Passenger safety must be the primary concern of all bus drivers. They must drive defensively to prevent accidents in all kinds of traffic and weather. For the comfort and safety of their passengers, they have to avoid sudden stops or quick turns that could jar anyone on the bus. The other duties of bus drivers depend on where they work and whether their passengers are schoolchildren, commuters, intercity travelers, or tourists.

As a bus driver, your hours will depend upon your particular job. Some drivers have part-time jobs working less than twenty hours per week, while others have a regular, full-time work schedule from week to week. A bus driver may also be on call-in status and have to work on short notice. Shift work and driving on weekends is common except for school bus drivers. With experience and seniority, drivers may be able to choose the routes they drive.

Qualifications and Training

In order to become a bus driver in the United States, you must meet qualifications and standards set by state and federal regulations. If you operate a bus made to transport sixteen or more passengers, federal regulations require you to hold a commercial driver's license (CDL) from the state where you live. To qualify for a CDL, you must pass a written test on rules and regulations and then demonstrate that you can operate a bus safely. In order to prepare for the CDL, you need to complete some behind-the-wheel training. A driver with a CDL must accompany trainees until they get this license.

Many states require bus drivers to be at least eighteen years old to drive within the state. Bus drivers who travel between states have to meet the Federal Motor Carrier Safety Regulations, which require a driver to be at least twenty-one years old and pass a physical examination every two years. These regulations are described in detail in Chapter 4. Some states have guidelines that exceed federal regulations that the driver must comply with in order to be licensed within that state.

In Canada, licensing is done on a provincial rather than national basis, and the requirements vary by province. In Ontario, for example, a bus driver needs a Class B, C, E, or F driver's license, while a Class 2 license is required elsewhere in Canada. Check with the transportation department in your province for details.

Beyond meeting licensing requirements, bus drivers need to have certain personal characteristics in order to handle this job. They need an even temperament and emotional stability because driving in heavy, fast-moving, or stop-and-go traffic and dealing with passengers—from schoolchildren to senior citizens—can be stressful. Drivers also need to have solid communication skills and know how to manage large groups of people.

Job Opportunities for Bus Drivers

More and more bus driving jobs will be available in the twenty-first century as demand for public transportation increases due to the growing school-age population and to environmental concerns. In recent years, many employers have had difficulty in finding qualified candidates to fill positions. In the future, the best opportunities will be for school bus driving jobs. However, employment of local and intercity drivers will increase as bus ridership grows.

Driving a School Bus

School bus drivers usually work only during the school year. Very few are employed during the summer or school holidays. Some drivers take on the additional job of driving students on field trips or to athletic events. School bus drivers work a split schedule in which they run a morning route to get students to school and an afternoon run to return the students to their homes. Some drivers may run a midday route to drop off and pick up kindergartners who are on a half-day schedule. It may be possible for school bus drivers to take their buses home with them instead of having to return the buses to a terminal or garage.

On the job, school bus drivers must be extremely cautious when children are getting on or off the bus. Plus, they must be able to control the children and enforce safety rules as well as the student conduct rules put in place by the school system. Another task is the preparation of weekly reports on the number of students transported, the number of runs completed, and the amount of fuel used. A supervisor sets time schedules and routes.

Becoming a School Bus Driver

In the United States, you need a commercial driver's license in order to drive a school bus. Expect also to take some training in driving a bus unless you have had experience driving vehicles larger than an automobile. Most school bus drivers complete between one and four weeks of driving instruction plus classroom training on state and local laws, regulations, and policies of operating school buses. In addition, they study safe driving practices, driver-pupil relations, first aid, the special needs of disabled students, and emergency evacuation procedures. School bus drivers must also learn about school system rules for discipline and conduct for bus drivers and the students they transport.

In Canada, school bus drivers need to have a high school diploma and a minimum of one year safe driving experience. Training includes up to three months of on-the-job training with some classroom instruction time. Throughout Canada, bus drivers need a special driver's license, but the specific class varies by province. In addition, school bus drivers may need an air brake endorsement and a first aid certificate.

Job Outlook and Earnings

You won't find it too difficult to get a job as a school bus driver because these jobs are usually plentiful due to their part-time status, the high turnover rate, and the minimal training requirements. In fact, you can expect more job openings to occur in the future as enrollment is predicted to grow in both elementary and secondary schools. Opportunities will be best in suburban areas where students generally ride school buses. In Canada, the demand for school bus drivers is lower because of fewer school-age children.

The average earnings for school bus drivers are about $12.00 per hour. What you make will vary by where you are employed. Some drivers earn just over $6.00 per hour, and others earn nearly $17.00 per hour. Canadian school bus drivers can expect to earn between C$9.18 and C$17.47. Because bus drivers do not work when school is not in session, they do not get vacation leave. However, they usually receive sick leave, and many are covered by health and life insurance and pension plans.

On the Job with a School Bus Driver

B. Kay Wohlford is a school bus driver for a large metropolitan school district with fifty-three schools and about thirty-two thousand students. Kay loves to drive and really enjoys children. When her two daughters, Heather and Monica, were school age, Kay decided it would be great to drive a bus for their school. Her day begins at 6 A.M., when she picks up elementary-age kids and takes them to school. Her first route ends by 9:30 A.M. At 11 A.M., Kay picks up morning kindergarten students and takes them to their homes. After finishing the kindergarten route, she goes to a high school to take more students home. In addition to her regular route, Kay may get an assignment to drive children home after their extracurricular activities, such as athletics practices. Her last route of the day is complete by 6 P.M.

Each morning before starting her bus route, Kay makes a safety inspection of the bus by checking the lights, windshield wipers, tire pressure, brakes, and flashers. She carefully inspects the bus from front to back. At first, Kay used a checklist during her inspection. With experience, she relies less on the checklist because her daily inspection has become an automatic part of her workday. At the end of the day, Kay sweeps the bus, turns articles left on the bus into the lost and found, and, most importantly, carefully checks the bus to make sure there are no sleeping children on it.

Training to Be a Driver. Kay has a Class B commercial driver's license with a passenger endorsement in order to drive a school bus. She spent ten hours in a classroom learning the ins and outs of driving a school bus as well as some basic first aid. Then Kay had to pass a written test over what she had learned in class. Next, an instructor taught her how to drive a bus. This included learning how to bleed the brakes and complete the bus safety checklist used before and after school bus routes. Finally, Kay had to pass a road test.

Driving a School Bus for Special-Needs Children

Janet Hively comes from a family of school bus drivers. Her father and sister have more than forty years of experience between them. It was her sister who told her about the position of driver for special-education students for a rural school corporation. When Janet started this job, she transported preschoolers to and from school; however, the program has steadily grown as more special-education students have been included in regular classrooms. Janet's passengers are now children from preschoolers through high school students who have a wide range of disabilities.

Janet's workday usually begins at about 6:15 A.M., when she does a pretrip check of her fifteen-passenger bus. She checks the oil, lights, tires, and flashers to be sure everything is in proper working order. Then Janet lets the bus warm up for about ten minutes before starting her 150-mile route so that it will be comfortable for the students.

On her first trip of the day, the bus is almost full because Janet drives thirteen students. Five are in wheelchairs and require the use of the wheelchair lift built into the bus. Susie, who has been her aide for several years, helps secure the students into the wheelchair section of the bus or into their seats—a task that can take up to five minutes for each student. These first riders are all dropped off at their various schools by 8:30 A.M. Next, Janet picks up nine preschoolers who have a variety of disabilities requiring Susie's help to seat them. After delivering the preschoolers to the school, Janet has a break for about forty minutes. She may use this time to check the bus for any problems before picking up one student who is only able to attend high school for two hours. After transporting this student to his home, it is time to pick up the preschoolers and return them to their homes. This run takes about forty-five minutes to complete.

For her last run of the day, Janet picks up the children from her first run and takes them to their homes. After dropping off the last rider, Janet checks every seat to be sure no children are still on board. Then, in preparation for the next day, she refuels her bus.

Training for the Job. Before Janet began driving this special-education route, she had to earn her commercial driver's license. First, she attended a state-mandated two-week training session. Then she rode with another driver for twelve hours, followed by twelve hours of driving with an instructor on board. Today, new drivers must complete a visual test in which they are required to identify forty points on the bus. They also must be able to identify and name parts such as the transmission, brake lines, air filter, and oil filter. This is to ensure that drivers are able to accurately communicate mechanical problems to supervisors and mechanics.

Janet has received special training in administering CPR as well as instruction in basic sign language so that she can communicate with the deaf children she transports. She has also been trained to help children who are on oxygen, have feeding tubes, or wear heart monitors. Some of this training is a result of her own initiative because it was not required by the school district. Janet believes in going the extra mile for her special passengers.

Career Pluses and Minuses. Janet finds the pay and insurance and retirement benefits offered by her employer to be good. The real plus of her career, however, is getting to know the children and their parents. Janet gives the children a great deal of attention in order to make them feel safe on her bus. As a result, a special bond has developed. Recently, Janet's family had a birthday party for her, and several of the students and their families attended the celebration. Most school bus drivers do not have the opportunity to know their riders this well.

This job has also given Janet a great rapport with the teachers of the children she transports. One teacher, especially, has given her solid advice on how to handle these special children effectively when they are riding on her bus. Janet believes that the teachers have made her a better bus driver.

Along with the positive aspects of this job are the negative ones. The weather can make the roads very dangerous and difficult to drive. Then there are the discourteous and reckless drivers, especially those who don't want to get stuck behind a bus, who make her job far more difficult. Another difficult situation arises when one of the children loses control of his or her bodily functions.

Driving a Local Transit Bus

Local transit bus drivers work within a city or suburban area. They begin their workdays by reporting to a terminal or garage where they stock up on all the supplies—such as tickets, transfers, and trip report forms—needed on the job. Few bus drivers now carry money, as passengers are expected to have the correct fare. Some local drivers may have to do a pretrip check of the bus to be sure it is safe to operate before going out on the route. And a few are responsible for making sure that their buses are clean, from washing windows to cleaning the bus interior.

As a local transit driver, you follow a regularly scheduled route and make several trips during your shift. You may need to stop every few blocks to pick up and discharge passengers. Local bus drivers are also expected to be at stops at the times printed in the official company schedule. This can be extremely difficult because of traffic, weather, problems with passengers, and mechanical breakdowns.

As you drive along your route, you will dispense tickets and transfers and may collect fares. You will also need to be knowledgeable about where passengers need to get off to go to businesses, parks, and other attractions. Furthermore, passengers expect you to know what buses they need to take to get to different locations. Besides these tasks, you often have to deal with passengers who are frail, unruly, or rude. At the same time, you are responsible for giving everyone from schoolchildren to senior citizens a safe trip. At the end of your workday, you need to submit reports about the number of trips made, route delays, mechanical difficulties, accidents, and any other problems that occurred.

Like school bus drivers, most local transit bus drivers have a regular work schedule. They usually work a five-day, forty-hour workweek. Some drivers may have to work weekends, evening shifts, or even after midnight. It also may be necessary for drivers to work a split shift, such as 6 A.M. to 10 A.M. and 3 P.M. to 7 or 8 P.M., in order to accommodate high ridership during commuter rush hours.

Qualifications and Training

Local transit bus companies look for drivers who are at least twenty-four years old, have a high school diploma, are able to read complex bus schedules, and have some previous bus or truck driving experience. A good driver will have excellent customer service skills, be courteous, communicate well with the passengers, and be able to manage a large group of people.

Local transit bus drivers must hold a commercial driver's license. Many companies offer training for their new drivers. This usually includes several weeks of classroom work with instruction in reading schedules, keeping records, and dealing with passengers in a professional manner. The behind-the-wheel training typically involves practicing maneuvers such as backing up, changing lanes, and turning. This is first done on a closed course and then later on the highway or streets. Drivers may also make trial runs without passengers to improve their driving skills and learn the routes. In smaller cities, trainees memorize and drive each of the runs operating out of their assigned garages. After completing their training, new drivers may be placed on a call-in status and have to work at any given time, especially on short notice. They are often assigned only part-time hours until they gain experience. As drivers get more seniority, they may request more appealing routes as well as schedules with weekends off.

Job Outlook and Earnings

Employment growth for local transit bus drivers in the United States and Canada is expected to be faster than the average for all occupations. This is because of the increasing popularity of mass transit due to congestion and rising fuel prices, as well as the demand for transit services in expanding portions of metropolitan areas. There may be competition for positions with more regular hours and steady driving routes. Only in a few areas where there are high wages and very attractive benefits is there intense competition for local bus driver jobs.

How much money you make as a local bus driver depends greatly on where you live. In larger cities, you can expect to earn up to $24.00 per hour. Overall, transit bus drivers in the United States earn between $10.74 and $19.31 an hour. Canadian drivers earn between C$18.00 and C$25.00 per hour.

On the Road with a Local Transit Bus Driver

It is thirty-five feet long, ten feet wide, and weighs 27,700 pounds empty. A local transit bus is big and powerful. It takes a well-trained professional like Brenda Benson to control it and be sure the passengers arrive at their destinations safely and on time. Brenda drives a bus for a company that provides transportation service to a city with 275,000 people. There are twelve routes and eighty full- and part-time drivers. More than 2.5 million rides were provided by her bus company in 2006.

Brenda began her career by driving a paratransit bus, which transports handicapped, elderly, and disabled people. After about eighteen months, Brenda was able to get a route driving a "big bus." Before going out on her own, Brenda completed a three-week training period. She drove the bus with an experienced driver supervising her. After the training period, Brenda was on her own. During her five years as a transit bus driver, she has driven seven different routes.

The drivers in this company bid for routes based on seniority. This is a common practice in most local transit companies. Because Brenda is one of the more senior drivers, she is usually able to get the routes she wants. She likes working the afternoon to evening shift. Most of the drivers work eight-hour days, five days a week. Because of her seniority, Brenda has been able to have weekends off. If she does work more than forty hours per week, she is paid time and a half.

A Typical Day on a Route. Brenda reports to work at 1 P.M. She relieves a driver whose day began at 5 A.M. Brenda makes an inspection of the bus before she starts her route. She walks around the bus, checking windshield wipers and tires and looking for damage. She checks the kneeler, which lowers the bus for easier access. She also checks to be sure the wheelchair lift works properly. If there are any problems, she calls the garage to request service or a change of buses. Then this road warrior is ready to roll.

Out on the route, Brenda doesn't handle money; passengers just put their coins or bills in the fare box. Although she doesn't have an official break, at the end of each loop, she usually has five to ten minutes, depending on the traffic. On busy days, she may not have time for a break, especially during peak rider times. Brenda's shift ends at 9:15 P.M., when she takes her bus back to headquarters. She walks through the bus to be sure there are no passengers. She also shuts down the fare box, turns off interior lights, and turns off the bus. Brenda then turns in her paperwork. Sometimes she has reports to fill out, such as accident reports, incident reports, or a defect sheet for bus repair.

Career Pluses and Minuses. Brenda appreciates that her job offers good benefits, including medical and dental insurance, paid vacations, and retirement. On the job, she likes being on her own for the entire workday as well as seeing her regular passengers each day. One of Brenda's stops during the day is to pick up a group of special-needs adults who are going home. Brenda says these passengers are "exceptionally kind and courteous" and a joy to have on the bus. Of course, there are negatives to this job, such as being stuck in traffic, dealing with passengers who don't have fares, worrying that an unsteady older passenger will fall, and not always having a break between runs. Driving on snow and ice is a challenge in itself, in addition to being aware of other drivers on the road. One of her biggest challenges is trying to give directions to people who have limited English skills or are hearing impaired. Sometimes the stress of always being on guard while driving can get to Brenda. Nevertheless, these negative things become more bearable when the adults give Brenda praise and compliments for her excellent driving abilities and she gets loving hugs from her littlest riders.

Driving an Intercity Bus

Intercity bus drivers transport passengers from city to city within a state or between different regions of the country. They may make only a single one-way trip to a distant city or a round-trip between cities each day. Drivers may stop at several small towns that are just a few miles apart or stop at large cities that are hundreds of miles apart. While some intercity drivers make extended trips of more than one day, there are strict federal guidelines limiting actual driving time. For instance, long-distance drivers may not work more than sixty hours in a seven-day period, and for every ten hours of driving, they must rest eight hours.

Intercity drivers work nights, weekends, and holidays and may spend nights away from home at company expense. Drivers with more seniority often have more regular hours during a week; others must be prepared to drive on short notice. Because intercity bus travel service tends to be seasonal, drivers can expect to work as many hours as regulations allow from May through August. During the off-season, some drivers with less seniority may get very few hours. They may even be furloughed and get no driving jobs for a period of time.

In early 2006, a new type of intercity bus service, Megabus, emerged that provides nonstop express service between several Midwestern cities. After one year, Megabus has fourteen cities included in its routes. Megabus offers fares as low as one dollar. These low fares and the nonstop service hold the promise of a quickly expanding industry that can successfully compete with airlines for short-trip business. The need for more intercity drivers for Megabus and other intercity companies will certainly grow.

Qualifications and Training

Intercity bus companies look for their drivers to have very similar qualifications to those of local transit drivers, including holding a commercial driver's license. Many intercity bus companies offer training for their new drivers. This usually includes two to eight weeks of classroom work and behind-the-wheel training. In the classroom, new drivers learn U.S. Department of Transportation and company rules, safety regulations, state and municipal driving regulations, and safe driving practices. They also learn how to handle record keeping and the appropriate way to deal with passengers. Canadian drivers complete similar training and must be aware of provincial or territorial rules and regulations.

Job Outlook and Earnings

Employment opportunities will be best for new intercity bus drivers who have driving experience. Because travelers often opt to make longer trips by plane or rail, employment will only increase as ridership does. Most growth in employment for intercity drivers will probably be in group charter travel, rather than scheduled intercity bus services.

The average hourly pay for intercity bus drivers in the United States is $14.30, with top pay being about $19.31 per hour. Canadian intercity bus drivers earn between C$17.87 to C$24.80 per hour. In both countries, their benefits may include paid health and life insurance, sick leave, and free bus rides on any of the routes of their line or system. Full-time drivers may receive as much as four weeks of vacation time annually.

On the Road with an Intercity Bus Driver

As a teenager, Lloyd Benedict liked to drive; however, he never imagined then that he would have a career as a bus driver. Instead, he thought he would become a jeweler. Unfortunately, he soon discovered that he would need a part-time job to supplement his income as a struggling jeweler. He saw an ad for a position as a school bus driver, applied for the job, and got it after attending a two-week course in order to get sufficient training and a license.

After working as a school bus driver for three years, Lloyd decided that he wanted to see more of the country and applied for a job as an intercity driver with Greyhound Lines. When he applied for this job many years ago, the position of driver for Greyhound was held in such high esteem that competition was intense. Only one in forty applicants was hired. Lloyd believes that he was able to get one of these positions because of his three years of experience as a school bus driver and his safe driving record.

After six weeks of company training, Lloyd became a Greyhound driver. Because routes in almost all bus companies are assigned by seniority, Lloyd was placed on the on-call board, which meant he had to be available twenty-four hours a day. He especially remembers being called at night to drive from San Francisco to Reno in a blizzard. As he gained seniority, Lloyd began to be able to choose his runs. His favorite was going from San Francisco to Fort Bragg, California, because it is so scenic. He also traveled frequently to Reno, Fresno, and San Luis Obispo. Most of his routes were completed in a day with only an occasional overnight stay.

As an intercity bus driver, Lloyd felt he had the same role as the captain of a ship. Once he left the bus terminal, he was responsible for everything that happened on the bus. He had to stop in isolated regions to pick up passengers and collect their fares, load and unload the luggage, as well as make sure that the passengers behaved in an orderly manner. The company also was a freight carrier, so he had to drop off packages in small towns.

Lloyd drove for Greyhound for seven years. He left this job after a bitter drivers' strike and later began driving a tour bus through the San Francisco Bay Area.

Driving a Motor Coach

Motor coach drivers conduct passengers on charter trips and sightseeing tours. Sightseeing trips can be one-day excursions through a city or extended trips covering several states. Multiday trips require drivers to be away for several days or possibly several weeks at a time.

The hours motor coach drivers spend on the job are dictated by the charter trips booked and the prearranged itinerary of tours. If you become a motor coach driver, you can expect to work any day and all hours of the day, including weekends and holidays. However, like all bus drivers, your actual hours on the job must be consistent with U.S. Department of Transportation or Canadian territorial or provincial rules and regulations.

Qualifications and Training

Motor coach drivers must hold a commercial driver's license and comply with the same federal, state, or provincial regulations as local transit and intercity drivers. A few companies may offer training; however, they usually look for and hire applicants who already have experience driving buses and need very little training.

Job Outlook and Earnings

Driving a charter bus or tour bus tends to be seasonal work, except in popular tourist spots that have visitors throughout the year. Drivers may work the maximum allowable hours during tourist season, which usually runs from May through August. During the off-season, drivers with less seniority may work a limited number of hours and even be furloughed. Motor coach drivers on average earn less than intercity bus drivers; however, they may also earn tips that substantially increase their incomes.

Driving a Motor Coach in San Francisco

After seven years as a Greyhound driver, Lloyd Benedict, whose career as an intercity driver was described earlier in this chapter, became a tour bus driver. Today, he is the number-two driver for a small tour bus company in San Francisco and is able to select which route he drives. On most days, he only works in the city. Occasionally, he drives out of town overnight when he does two- or three-day tours out of San Francisco to Yosemite, Reno, or down the coast to the Monterey Peninsula. He usually drives a very well-appointed forty-foot bus that has a restroom, relieving him of the necessity of making unexpected stops for passengers. The bus has a capacity of fifty to fifty-five passengers; however, groups vary in size and are often smaller.

A Typical Day's Work. Lloyd's day begins when he arrives at the bus yard at 7:45 A.M. He is very familiar with his bus, since he drives the same bus every day. His first tasks are to fuel the bus and do a pretrip check according to a form that he fills out each day. On the day described here, he drove to a hotel where he was to pick up a French tour group at 9 A.M. He arrived early and used the time to study for a course that he was taking. Shortly, the guide arrived and talked to him about the sights the tour group would see. Lloyd jotted down the route he would follow once the group was aboard the bus. As the guide described the sights of San Francisco, Lloyd drove by some tourist spots and stopped at others for visits and photo opportunities. At the end of this half-day tour, he drove the group across the Golden Gate Bridge to Sausalito, where the tourists had lunch before embarking on a ferry ride on the bay.

Lloyd then returned to San Francisco to pick up another tour group at a hotel to take them to the airport. He loaded their luggage aboard the bus and unloaded it at the airport. Once he left this group, he had some wait time before picking up a new tour group at the airport and taking them to a hotel. Again, he handled the loading and unloading of the luggage by himself. His day was over at this point, and he returned the bus to the company terminal.

Typically, Lloyd works from eight to ten hours a day and drives three or four tour groups around the Bay Area. In the high tourist season, which is May to October, he works fourteen- to sixteen-hour days six days a week. It is essential for him to do this in order to compensate for the income that he loses during the months when tourism is slack. Although Lloyd works long days, the law prevents him from driving more than ten hours of that time. The rest of the time is wait time, for which he is paid.

Career Pluses and Minuses. The greatest thing about driving a tour bus, according to Lloyd, is that you are working with tourists who are looking forward to having fun. Also, you are able to be home almost every night. This is one career in which you do not need more than a high school education and very little training to make a decent living. Lloyd believes that the major negative to this career is the long hours he must work in the high tourist season. It is also becoming increasingly difficult to drive in the traffic of the San Francisco Bay Area.

Driving a Charter Bus in Indiana

Hank Hanson is a driver for the Landmark Charter Coach Service in Fort Wayne, Indiana. While Hank has not always driven buses, he has usually had a career that let him be a road warrior. As a teenager, he drove a milk truck. Then, while he was in the service, Hank was behind the wheel of a truck pulling guns as well as a fuel truck. Hank has also been a driver for a short-haul trucking company and later became its terminal manager, overseeing forty-five drivers. After leaving the trucking company, Hank started a trash collection business, which he built into a successful multitruck operation.

In the back of his mind, Hank never relinquished his boyhood dream of driving a bus. An unexpected delay in a Greyhound bus station gave him the opportunity to begin pursuing this dream. He saw an ad for a job as a Greyhound bus driver and decided to apply. Hank filled out an application, was accepted, and soon was attending a six-week company driving school. After completing the training, he began driving for Greyhound. He didn't have a regular route but was on an extra board, which meant that he could be called at any time to drive. After a short stint as a Greyhound driver, Hank moved to a job driving charters with a small four-bus company.

Responsibilities with the Charter Bus Company. Besides driving charter routes for Landmark Charter Coach Service, Hank is the company's safety supervisor. In this role, he takes prospective drivers out in a bus and grades how they drive, looking at how they handle turns and drive on city streets and interstates. A high grade will earn drivers a recommendation for employment. Hank knows the buses very well and frequently helps the company owner solve mechanical problems reported by drivers. Together, they keep this small fleet of buses running and on the road. Landmark currently has one fifty-seven-passenger bus, two forty-seven-passenger buses, and one thirty-five-passenger bus. In addition, Hank attends seminars given by bus manufacturers to learn more about handling new buses and making repairs.

When Hank goes out on the road with a charter, there are usually about forty people in the group. Most of his trips are short runs completed in one day. His longest charter was a nineteen-day tour of the western half of the United States. The group visited places like Yellowstone in Wyoming and the Badlands in South Dakota. He also traveled with the United States Women's Volleyball Team for fourteen days.

In his job as a charter bus driver, Hank takes many senior citizen groups on one-day trips within the state. He also transports many groups to sporting events and frequently drives high school, college, and professional sport teams to their games. Occasionally, Hank drives a charter for celebrities and has had both Marie Osmond and the Beach Boys aboard his bus.

A Typical Charter Trip. When Hank drives a tour group on a one-day trip, he gets his bus at the company's terminal, or it is delivered to him by one of the company's other drivers. Most groups have an escort who meets with him to discuss the route and time schedule. On the bus, the escort oversees the group's activities.

For a one-day charter trip of four hundred miles round-trip to a specialty basket manufacturing and sales company in Ohio, Hank began driving at about 6 A.M. The group reached its destination at about 9 A.M. Then he transported some of the group to a nearby town for additional touring. Most of the time between a charter's arrival and departure at a destination is downtime for Hank, although the group escort may invite him to go with the group on the planned activity. Usually, he stays with the bus in case anyone in the group requires transportation to a special destination. Hank may use this time to nap because his days can be very long. During the return trip, the Ohio group stopped at a restaurant for dinner, and the trip was not completed until 10 P.M.

Career Pluses and Minuses. Hank really enjoys driving and traveling with charter groups. While he used to do more long-distance driving, he now drives shorter one-day trips and still sees lots of great things within the area. He especially enjoys talking with the passengers and getting to know them as they travel. His favorite trip is a tour to Branson, Missouri. On this trip, he joins with the group in attending shows. Then he enjoys the added fun after the shows when the performers frequently get on the bus to greet and talk with the tour. Hank has also had some unpleasant experiences when people on charters have engaged in fights that have actually damaged the bus.

For More Information

In order to learn more about jobs for bus drivers in your area, contact local transit systems, intercity bus lines, school systems, and the local office of the state employment service. You also should check the classified ads in newspapers.

For school information contact:

National School Transportation Association
113 South West Street, Fourth Floor
Alexandria, VA 22314
www.yellowbuses.org

Local transit bus driving information can be obtained from:

American Public Transit Association
1666 K Street NW
Washington, DC 20006
www.apta.com

Transportation Association of Canada
2323 St. Laurent Boulevard
Ottawa, ON K1G 4J8
Canada
www.tac-atc.ca

You can learn about driving a motor coach from:

United Motorcoach Association
113 South West Street, Fourth Floor
Alexandria, VA 22314
www.uma.org

American Bus Association (North America)
700 Thirteenth Street NW, Suite 575
Washington, DC 20005
www.buses.org

Ontario Motor Coach Association
4141 Yonge Street, Suite 306
Toronto, ON M2P 2A8
Canada
www.omca.com

CHAPTER SIX

Driving for Delivery Services

Not too many years ago, almost all letters, advertisements, and packages were delivered to homes and businesses in the United States and Canada by their respective government postal services. This is no longer true. Today, giant national and international delivery services are also picking up and delivering billions of documents and packages from drop boxes, businesses, and residences and delivering them to addresses across town and almost everywhere in both countries as well as throughout the world. Plus, there are smaller national, regional, state, and even city delivery services. All of these delivery services, as well as the government postal services, offer quick and convenient weekday services, and some also have weekend and all-hour services. Your local mail carrier leaves letters, bills, advertisements, and packages in your mailbox or at your door. Delivery companies leave documents and packages on doorsteps and in offices.

In working for the postal service, the major opportunities to be behind the wheel are for rural carriers and those who transport mail between post offices and distribution centers. A career with a delivery service presents more opportunities to be a driver. Many offer a full day on the road making lots of stops for deliveries and pickups. Delivery service drivers are behind the wheel in cars, vans, or trucks. Some may even be on bicycles.

83

....

Postal Services

For centuries, the only way that people had to exchange ideas with people in distant places was by the different postal systems that developed throughout the world. This held true until the telegraph, telephone, radio, and television were invented. Now, of course, the Internet lets people everywhere communicate almost instantly with others just about everywhere on earth. Still, postal services remain an important means of communication. These services bring letters, magazines, advertisements, and packages to homes and businesses throughout North America every day.

The United States Postal Service

A postal service was created by the Continental Congress in 1775, and Benjamin Franklin was appointed the first postmaster general. Prior to that time, the postal service was a monopoly run by an appointee of the King of England. The colonists were very unhappy with this system, as their mail could be opened and read to check their loyalty to the crown. When the Continental Congress established a mail service in 1782, it was decreed that private letters could not be opened by the postal authorities. Then in 1789, Congress passed the first postal act establishing the Post Office Department. This department was replaced with the United States Postal Service as an independent government agency in 1971 in order to provide the country with a more efficient and timely mail service. Since 1982, the postal service has accepted no public subsidies.

The Canada Post Corporation

In 1753, Benjamin Franklin became the deputy postmaster general for the British colonies in North America. He was dismissed from this job in 1774 because of his role in the American Revolution. Until 1851, the Canadian postal system was administered by the British government when its operation was turned over to the

provinces. After confederation in 1868, the post office was operated by the federal government until 1981, when its operation was
turned over to the Canada Post Corporation.

The Job of Mail Carriers

Mail carriers cover their routes on foot, by vehicle, or a combination of both. In some urban and most rural areas, they use a car
or small truck. Although the postal service provides vehicles to
city carriers, most rural carriers use their own automobiles.

The carriers do far more than deliver mail: they also collect
money for postage-due and COD (cash on delivery) fees, and they
obtain signed receipts for registered, certified, and insured mail. If
you become a city carrier, you could also have very specialized
duties. You might deliver only certain types of mail or just pick up
mail from mail collection boxes. As a rural carrier, you should
expect to provide a wider variety of services than city carriers.
These carriers may sell stamps and money orders and register, certify, and insure parcels and letters.

Mail carriers usually begin their days in the post office, where
they arrange the mail in delivery sequence. Fortunately, auto-
mated equipment has reduced sorting time, allowing carriers to
spend more time out on their routes delivering mail. At the end of
the day, drivers of postal vehicles return them to the post office.

Working Conditions

It is not always easy to be a mail carrier. During peak delivery
times, such as before the winter holidays, mail carriers frequently
have to work overtime. Their regular week, however, is forty hours
over a five-day period. Carriers also have to deliver mail in all
kinds of weather, from cold, snowy winter days to hot summer
days. Plus, driving a postal vehicle requires the driver to do stop-
and-start driving and to watch very carefully for other drivers and
pedestrians, especially before and after making deliveries. There is
also considerable reaching in this job in order to get the mail from

postal vehicles into every box on the route. And at times, mail carriers need to leave their vehicles in order to deliver the mail to certain addresses. While carriers often begin work early in the morning, they have the advantage of being through by early afternoon. Most mail carriers particularly like having a job in which their workdays are relatively free of direct supervision.

Job Qualifications

To become a mail carrier in the United States, you must be at least eighteen years old and a citizen or have been granted permanent resident-alien status. Qualification for the job is based on a written examination that measures speed and accuracy at checking names and numbers and the ability to memorize mail distribution procedures. You must also pass a physical examination and drug test and may be asked to show that you can lift and handle mail sacks weighing seventy pounds. In addition, you need a valid driver's license, a good driving record, and a passing grade on a road test.

To begin the process of becoming a mail carrier in the United States, you need to contact the post office or mail processing center where you want to work to find out when an examination will be given. After an examination, all of the applicants' names are listed in order of their examination scores. Veterans who were honorably discharged have five points added to their scores, and those who were wounded in combat or are disabled have ten points added. When a vacancy occurs, the appointing officer chooses one of the top three applicants; the rest of the names remain on the list to be considered for future openings until their eligibility expires—usually two years after the examination date.

To become a mail carrier in Canada, it is recommended that you have a high school diploma. You will also have to pass Canada Post's mail carrier test, have a valid driver's license and good references, and pass a security clearance.

Training and Advancement

As a mail carrier, you can expect to be trained on the job by experienced workers. Many post offices offer classroom instruction on safety and defensive driving. Whenever new equipment or procedures are introduced, you will receive additional instruction from another postal worker or a training specialist.

Mail carriers often begin on a part-time, flexible basis and advance to regular or full-time work in order of seniority as vacancies occur. Carriers can look forward to obtaining preferred routes as their seniority increases or to getting high-level jobs, such as carrier technician. They can advance to supervisory positions on a competitive basis.

Job Outlook and Earnings

There is keen competition for jobs as mail carriers because the number of applicants always exceeds the number of openings. Although mail volume will increase and partnership with express delivery companies will increase the volume of mail to be delivered, several trends are expected to increase carrier productivity and lead to slower than average growth for these workers. In the United States, there will be a small decline in mail carriers through 2014.

The best opportunities will be in rural areas and suburbs. While the number of postal workers declined in Canada during the 1990s, employment opportunities are expected to be good through 2011.

The median annual earnings of mail carriers in the United States exceed $44,000. Plus, those who drive their own cars on routes are reimbursed for mileage.

In Canada, the median salary exceeds C$34,000 a year. Mail carriers in both the United States and Canada enjoy a variety of employer-provided benefits similar to those enjoyed by other federal government workers.

Behind the Wheel as a Mail Carrier

Cesar Vargas delivers mail in a suburban area. He is a full-time regular with five different routes. One of these routes is a walking route in the business district of a small town, and the others are traveled behind the wheel of a small half-ton truck. Cesar works five days a week, taking over when the regular route carrier has a day off. He would prefer to have his own driving route, but the opportunity to do so will only occur when someone retires or new routes are established. Then, being fortunate enough to get one's own route is based on seniority. Cesar believes that he will have his own route within a year because many new subdivisions are being built, necessitating new routes, and he has considerable seniority, having worked at this job for seven years.

Cesar started as a part-time, flexible worker at the post office. This is not an uncommon way to get one's foot in the door in this career as there is so much competition for postal jobs. He would work anywhere from twenty to forty hours a week. It took Cesar two and a half years to become a regular employee.

Today, he typically works fifty to fifty-six hours a week, which gives him considerable work above the typical forty-hour week. He welcomes this work because overtime pay is one and one-half times regular hourly wages. During the December holiday rush, there is no limit to the number of hours he may be required to work. For the rest of the year, overtime is limited to sixteen hours a week.

Becoming a Carrier. In order for Cesar to become a carrier in the area where he wished to work, he took the postal exam along with about three thousand other people. Because he passed the test, his name was placed on a list to be called when a vacancy occurred. It took him a year to get his first position as a part-time, flexible postal worker. Cesar had to have a driver's license and a good driving record and to receive a passing grade on a road test to get a job driving a motorized route. If he gets too many speeding or traffic violations on his state driver's license, he could be suspended or even lose his job.

Cesar was trained for a full day on the four-cylinder vehicle that he would drive. The training consisted of a class and video. When he got a new, more powerful vehicle, he had to be trained on that as well.

On the Job. Cesar starts his workday at 7:30 A.M. after checking in on the computerized job clock. Then, he picks up his keys and goes out to inspect his vehicle for any possible problems. Next, it's back to the post office to spend close to three hours sorting mail into cases in the exact order of his route. Depending on the route, he sorts mail for between 300 to 380 customers. Every letter must be placed in the correct spot in one of the cases that will go in his truck or, for his walking route, in bags. Cesar also has to indicate the addresses on the route where he will drop off packages.

Once all the sorting is completed, and it does have to be done rapidly, Cesar puts all the mail and packages in a hamper, rolls them out to his truck, and loads it for his driving routes. Then it's time to drive out to his route and begin delivering the mail. Because he has many customers and their homes are not close together, he may not be done until 5 or 5:30 in the afternoon. Cesar drives about five miles per hour between homes. He only increases his speed when he needs extra momentum to climb the hills.

At each stop, Cesar fingers through several cases to be sure he has all the letters, magazines, advertisements, and packages for that address. He has developed a system to this work that enables him to deliver the mail quickly. (Each carrier devises a system that works the easiest for him or her.) While most of his workday on the route is spent driving, Cesar frequently has to jump out of the truck to leave a package at a door.

A Good Job. Cesar especially likes this job because it pays well because he is able to earn so much overtime pay. He also appreciates the generous benefits this job offers. He likes the fact that he is out driving most of his workday. He especially enjoys the scenery on the routes that take him up in the hills. Plus, he appreciates the fact that there is no pressure from a supervisor as he goes about traveling his routes. The only downside of this job is that his vehicle can get hot on warm summer days—often reaching above ninety degrees in the area where he works. Nevertheless, he believes that being a mail carrier is an ideal job for people who love to be behind the wheel.

Worldwide Express Delivery Companies

Every year, businesses as well as people expect quicker and easier access to letters, documents, and goods. They also want to have more information about when something was shipped and when it will arrive. Filling this need are huge delivery services—each delivering more than a million documents and packages around the world every day. These companies have developed extremely sophisticated delivery systems enabling them to deliver shipments overnight. At the heart of all these services are drivers of delivery trucks—those who initially pick up shipments and those who deliver them to customers who may be ten miles or three thousand miles away. Within every one of these large companies, there are thousands of positions for road warriors who want to spend their days on the move.

DHL

Three California entrepreneurs (Adrian Dalsey, Larry Hillblom, and Robert Lynn) formed DHL in 1969 as a service between San Francisco and Hawaii. The company rapidly grew, initiating service to the Philippines, Japan, Hong Kong, and other destinations in the Pacific Basin. This was followed by expansion to Europe, Latin America, the Middle East, and Africa. In 1986, DHL was the first company to bring international air express services to the People's Republic of China. Today, the company offers service to 120,000 destinations in more than 220 countries and territories and has more than 450 hubs, warehouses, and terminals.

FedEx

Founder Frederick W. Smith started Federal Express to overcome the tremendous problems that existed in 1971 in getting packages and other airfreight delivered within a day or two. On its first night of operation, the company delivered 186 packages to twenty-five cities in the United States. Today, the company's average daily volume is more than 6.5 million shipments for express, ground, freight, and expedited delivery services. It also serves more than 220 countries and territories. It has a fleet of more than seventy thousand motorized vehicles.

UPS

Nineteen-year-old Jim Casey borrowed $100 from a friend in 1907 to start the American Messenger Company, which he ran with other teenagers and his brother. The company specialized in delivering packages for retail stores. In 1919, the company, which had earlier merged with a competitor, became known as United Parcel Service. In the 1950s, the company began expanding beyond delivering for retail stores to become a giant delivery service. Its daily delivery volume is now 15.6 million packages and documents. The company currently serves more than two hundred countries and territories as well as every address in North America and Europe. The company has more than ninety-four thousand package cars, vans, tractors, and motorcycles. Almost all of the senior management of UPS began their careers as package sorters, drivers, or administrative assistants.

Job Outlook and Earnings

The number of job opportunities for drivers continues to increase at large delivery services because they are handling a greater number of documents and packages each year. While these delivery services employ thousands of drivers, competition for these jobs is very intense. Most drivers start as package handlers. In the United States, the median annual earnings for drivers exceed $47,000. In Canada, the median annual earnings exceed C$48,000.

On the Move with a UPS Driver

While Shane Barlow was still in college, he began his career with UPS loading delivery trucks. He worked full-time at this job, which began at 3:30 in the morning, and then he attended college at night. Because this job pays well, many college students work as loaders and then go on to other positions in the company. UPS likes to promote workers from within the company because they already know so much about how it operates. After several years of loading trucks, Shane had the opportunity to become a part-time driver, substituting for regular drivers. His experience as a loader helped him get this job because he knew how to place shipments within a truck. Shane's day as a substitute driver would begin at 8:30 in the morning after he had finished his job as a loader, and his job might not end until 5:30 or 6:30 in the evening. Sometimes, he worked a fourteen- or fifteen-hour day.

To become a UPS driver, Shane needed to obtain a Department of Transportation card. To get this card, he had to have a regular driver's license and a clean driving record and to pass a physical examination. He also had to demonstrate to the company that he could lift 150 pounds using a handcart and could move reasonably fast. Once Shane was approved as a driver, he was given three days of training.

Driving a Regular Route. Before Shane graduated from college, he had become a full-time driver with UPS. At first, he did not have a regular route and floated between different routes. However, as he gained seniority, he bid for the route that he has today. There are close to 140 drivers on routes working out of the center where he begins and ends his day. Shane's route is primarily in a residential area in a suburb; however, he also stops at a few businesses. He has been on this route for several years. In a typical day, he drives from fifty-five to seventy-five miles.

Shane's delivery truck is loaded between 3 and 8:15 A.M. All the deliveries that must be made before 10:30 A.M. are placed up front in the cab. Shane immediately looks at them and decides on the best possible route to ensure that these shipments are delivered on time. After completing these deliveries, he reviews the other shipments and rearranges the shelves so that each delivery can easily be found as he starts out on his route. He has found that the same addresses tend to get most of the deliveries. At each delivery stop, Shane has to be very careful that the truck is safely parked. Then he finds the right shipment, scans it into a handheld computer, exits the truck on the right side, and makes the delivery. Most shipments are simply left at the door. For a few, he needs to record signatures electronically. When he returns to the truck, Shane enters into the computer the pertinent facts about the delivery so that UPS has an accurate record of when, where, and to whom the shipment was delivered. Rather than having to type in most of this data, he simply presses certain buttons on the computer.

During the course of the workday, Shane makes from 170 to 190 delivery stops and approximately five to ten pickups that have been called in. Some drivers whose routes are in more densely populated areas make only seventy to ninety stops a day but will deliver more pieces than Shane does. Drivers who deliver primarily to businesses may also stop at the same addresses every day to pick up shipments.

When Shane has delivered every package on his truck, he returns the vehicle to the hub. A day typically ends at 7:30 P.M. Throughout the day, he has been on the move. He believes that this career is a good choice for those who want to spend most of their workday behind the wheel.

Career Advice. Shane wants prospective drivers to understand that this career involves hard work. He points out that drivers must be energetic as deliveries need to be made quickly. Plus, days can be long because drivers are expected to finish their routes, so working overtime is part of the job. He rarely works less than ten hours a day and may work twelve or more. Besides being a safe driver, Shane says it is very important for drivers to have a good sense of direction.

Smaller National, Regional, and Local Delivery Services

The job of delivering documents, packages, and freight is not just handled by the extremely large national and international delivery services and the postal service. There are many smaller companies offering delivery services throughout the United States and Canada. These companies may work with other smaller delivery services in order to reach every destination. They offer a wide range of same-day delivery services, including messenger, courier, and distribution services for clients consisting of small local firms to large national corporations.

Besides regional delivery services that handle shipments in several states, most large cities and metropolitan areas also have delivery services. Much of their work involves same-day or overnight pickup and delivery. They also deliver shipments to airports and pick up shipments at the airport for delivery. A few offer additional services, such as crating and storage. These companies give road warriors the opportunity to drive trucks, vans, pickups, and cars in mostly part-time and some full-time jobs.

Messengers like these jobs because they offer so much flexibility. They can work as much as they want. How much they earn naturally depends on how much they work. Many students have actually put themselves through college by working at small delivery services. Typically, these messengers are paid a percentage, usually 45 to 50 percent, of the amount the firm receives for a delivery. They can earn from $300 to more than $800 a week depending on how much they work.

Job Outlook and Earnings

Jobs at local and regional delivery services are expected to increase about as rapidly as the average for all occupations through 2014. How many jobs there will be in any year depends on the state of the economy. In the United States, the median annual salary for drivers at these services is more than $33,000. In Canada, the median annual salary is close to C$30,000. Drivers working for private firms will earn slightly more.

Bay Area Delivery

The goal of Bay Area Delivery in Benicia, California, is to "create dependability and confidence with your deliveries." The company offers same-day delivery and handles items that weigh from one to five thousand pounds in an area extending from the state capital of Sacramento to Santa Cruz on the Pacific Ocean (a distance of about 150 miles). The company has a courier component that delivers documents and packages and a freight side that delivers kitchen cabinets to homes that are being built or remodeled.

Delivery work is always done at a fast pace and can be exciting, especially when there is a medical emergency and the driver has to pick up a part for a CAT scanner and rush it to the airport to catch a certain flight. Of course, every day there is last-minute work, especially from graphic artists who want to get their work to customers by the end of the business day.

Bay Area Delivery is owned by Robert and Pat Clarenbach. Robert works in the office eight to ten hours a day handling various administrative responsibilities. This is an on-time, on-call business that operates around the clock, 365 days a year. When office hours are over, calls are routed to an off-hour dispatcher, who contacts drivers to handle urgent requests for pickups and deliveries. The busiest time of the day for the company is between 8 A.M. and 2 P.M. as 90 percent of the calls come in during this time. When a call comes in, one of the dispatchers answers it, writes down the delivery details, and dispatches a driver to the location for the pickup. They communicate with the drivers by phones and two-way radios.

Working as a Driver. The drivers who deliver documents and packages for Bay Area Delivery can hang around the office waiting for an assignment, but most are at home or in their own cars, pickups, and vans or in company vehicles handling deliveries or waiting for another job assignment. These drivers typically start their workdays between 7:30 A.M. and 8 A.M. and are usually done by 2 P.M. However, because they work for a company that operates twenty-four hours a day, they may make deliveries at all hours of the day and night.

On an average day, a driver will travel between 80 and 120 miles. Besides driving, the drivers have to load and unload the shipments and complete paperwork at each stop. This is a job in which individual drivers have a great deal of freedom. They choose the routes that they take to make deliveries and can usually take time off when they wish. For road warriors who do not wish to drive a regular route, this job presents an opportunity to travel to different areas each day.

Company drivers who work on the freight side of this delivery company work each day from 7:30 A.M. to 4 P.M. driving twenty-four-foot trucks. The trucks are loaded in the morning with kitchen cabinets of varying sizes. Then the driver and a helper make at least four and as many as eight deliveries during the day. Together, they unload the cabinets at each stop.

A New Type of Delivery Service

With so many families having two wage earners, it is helpful for them to have products—especially groceries, health and beauty aids, and office supplies—delivered right to their homes. Doing so is very easy as these products can typically be chosen on the Internet for home delivery. One of these companies is Peapod, which delivers to fifteen hundred zip codes and more than twelve million households in East Coast metropolitan areas and in Chicago. Within most metropolitan areas, there are several companies offering these delivery services. Businesses also use specialized services to obtain office supplies. Each of these services has jobs for those who want to be on the move throughout the workday.

Courier and Messenger Services

Local and regional delivery services make some of the same types of deliveries that are done by courier and messenger services. However, messenger services usually concentrate on delivering smaller shipments in a limited area. By sending a shipment by messenger, the sender ensures that it reaches its destination on the same day—sometimes even within the hour. Typically, messenger services are used to transport original and legal documents, blueprints and other oversize materials, large multipage documents, and securities. They also pick up and deliver medical samples, specimens, and other materials that must be delivered in a hurry.

On the job, messengers receive their instructions either by reporting to their offices in person, by telephone, or by two-way radio. They then pick up the item and carry it to its destination. After a delivery is made, they check with their offices to receive instructions about the next delivery. Consequently, they spend most of the working day in a vehicle, either their own or one the company provides. In some major urban areas, deliveries are made by bicycle or on foot.

Job Outlook and Earnings

The employment of couriers and messengers is expected to decline through 2014 even though there will be an increasing volume of parcels, business documents, promotional materials, and other written materials to be delivered. This occupation is being adversely affected by the more widespread use of technologies for electronic information handling such as e-mail and fax. However, couriers and messengers will still be needed to transport materials that cannot be sent electronically, such as blueprints and oversized materials. Also, they will still be needed by medical and dental laboratories and doctor and dentist offices to pick up and deliver medical samples, specimens, and other materials.

Messengers who work for delivery services may charge a fee for each item they pick up and deliver. Others work by the hour. The median annual earnings of couriers and messengers in the United States is slightly more than $20,000 a year, with the highest 10 percent earning above $30,000 a year. In Canada, the median annual earnings are above C$30,000 a year. Some messengers receive additional income through tips.

For More Information

To get more information about employment as a mail carrier, you should contact your local post office or a state or provincial employment service office. They will be able to supply you with details about entrance examinations and specific employment opportunities for mail carriers.

The large express transportation companies provide a wealth of information about their companies as well as employment opportunities on their websites. You may wish to visit the following sites:

- DHL: www.dhl-usa.com
- FedEx: www.fedex.com
- UPS: www.ups.com

The easiest way to find jobs with smaller regional and local delivery services is to conduct an online search for the companies that are in the area where you would like to work and to visit their websites. Newspaper ads and websites for job seekers will also direct you to prospective employers. Information about job opportunities for couriers and messengers may be obtained from local employers and local offices of the state employment service as well as newspaper ads and online employment websites. Besides working for messenger services, there are jobs for messengers at mail-order firms, banks, printing and publishing firms, utility companies, retail stores, and other large firms.

CHAPTER SEVEN

Driving Emergency and Public Safety Vehicles

People depend on police officers, firefighters, and paramedics and emergency medical technicians (EMTs) to save their lives. Police officers and firefighters also have the responsibility of protecting property. In handling the important duties of these occupations, the need to arrive at an emergency scene as rapidly and safely as possible is essential. It's the same story for ambulance drivers involved in transporting sick or injured people. Plus, animal control officers spend their days patrolling for stray animals as well as responding to animal emergencies. Working in any one of these careers will let you spend all or part of your day on the move while providing a valuable service to others.

Police Officers on the Move

Police, sheriff, and highway patrol officers enforce motor vehicle laws and regulations. At the scene of an accident, they may direct traffic, give first aid, or call for emergency equipment. In addition, they respond to other calls for service. Police agencies are usually organized into geographic districts, with the officers assigned to a specific area. They may be alone in their vehicles, but often they patrol with a partner, especially in high crime areas.

Police work can be very dangerous. It can also be extremely stressful—police officers often encounter death and suffering from accidents and criminal behavior. While officers are usually scheduled to work forty-hour weeks, overtime is very common. Plus, shift work is necessary because police protection must be provided around the clock.

Qualifications and Training

Civil service regulations govern the appointment of most police officers in the United States. Candidates must be U.S. citizens, usually at least twenty years old, and must meet rigorous physical and personal qualifications. Eligibility for appointment typically depends on performance in competitive written examinations and previous education and experience. In most police departments, a high school education is required; however, many require a year or two of college. State agencies typically require a college degree. It is also essential to have such personal characteristics as honesty, sound judgment, integrity, and a personal sense of responsibility. Most applicants are subjected to background checks, drug testing, and lie-detector tests.

In Canada, the requirements for becoming a police officer are equally demanding. Most recent candidates have a community college diploma, with three in ten holding a college degree.

Before police officers are given their first assignments, they usually go through a period of training. In state and large local departments, training is usually within the agency's police academy, often for twelve to fourteen weeks. In Canada, there is typically a three- to six-month training period. Before being given an actual assignment, recruits work with an experienced officer learning the ins and outs of everyday police work.

Job Outlook and Earnings

Working as a police officer is attractive to many because the job is challenging and involves much personal responsibility. Plus, at many agencies, it is possible to retire with a pension after twenty-five or thirty years of service and then pursue a second career. For these reasons, competition for jobs is keen, except in rural areas and small towns in the United States. The employment of police officers is expected to grow about as fast as the average for all occupations in the United States through 2014. In Canada, your prospects for becoming a police officer are only rated as fair, with the number of job seekers likely to match the number of job openings.

Median annual earnings of police and sheriff's patrol officers in the United States exceed $45,000, while those working in state agencies have median annual earnings of more than $48,000. In Canada, the hourly wages for police officers are above the national average at more than C$25 per hour. Police officers also receive such common benefits as paid vacation, sick leave, and medical and life insurance, as well as an allowance for uniforms.

On the Move with a Police Officer

Choose to become a police officer who patrols for a city, county, or state, and you have chosen a job that will put you on the move throughout your shift. Bryan Musgrove, a county patrol officer, actually spends more than 90 percent of his work time in a car. At the start of a shift, he reports to his assigned station for roll call and to be updated on new regulations and any outstanding crimes from the prior shifts, as well as suspects and vehicles to look for throughout the shift. Bryan then gets in his patrol car and begins traveling around his assigned zone.

Traveling by himself in his vehicle, Bryan answers any 911 calls in his zone, enforces traffic laws, and patrols neighborhoods. He is never sure what will happen out on the road during his shift. Throughout the day, he keeps a record of his activities, to be turned in at the end of his shift when he returns to the station for debriefing. During Bryan's six-days-on, three-days-off schedule, he works two different zones in the county. While Bryan finds his career extremely fulfilling because of the positive impact that his job has on the community, he is not enthusiastic about the shift hours that he must work at times.

Career Advice. Bryan recommends taking classes in law and criminal justice to see if you will enjoy a career in law enforcement. He also advises young people considering a career like his to take part in a Police Explorer Program as an introduction to police work. And to get a picture of what it would be like to be a patrol officer, he suggests doing a ride along with a local police officer in order to see firsthand exactly what is involved in this career.

Behind the Wheel with a State Highway Patrol Officer

Officer Julianne Burke is a state highway patrol officer who always wanted to go into law enforcement. While working at a desk job to pay for college, she often looked out the window and saw highway patrol officers cruising down the road. Not wanting to have a job in a cubicle for the rest of her life, she applied to become a highway patrol officer in her state. After completing a basic application, Julianne was invited to take a civil service test, which began the application process. Then she had to pass a physical agility test that was relatively easy for her, except for the running. The next step was for her to fill out a very lengthy packet with details about every place she had lived and with whom she had lived, as well as information about all her previous jobs. She was then assigned to a background investigator who checked the accuracy of this information. Julianne also had to take a voice stress analysis test to verify the accuracy of this information. During her final interview with the background investigator, she was offered a place in the highway patrol academy. She accepted the invitation and enrolled in the academy after graduating from college. It took about a year for Julianne to be accepted by the state agency from the day she filled out the application.

Starting Her Career. Julianne spent six months at the academy learning how to be a state highway patrol officer. During that time, she had to live at the academy, except on weekends. The curriculum included learning such things as the vehicle code, penal code, and emergency driving and law enforcement techniques.

Five days after her graduation from the academy, Julianne reported to her assigned office. She then did in-field training with four different officers learning how to apply the skills she learned in the academy to her new job. Once her training was completed, she began patrolling in her own patrol car.

On the Job. Julianne currently works the swing shift from 2 P.M. to 10 P.M. There is considerable potential for overtime beyond the forty hours that she works each week. In fact, she can generally work as much overtime as she wants. Additionally, she routinely has to go to traffic court. During a typical shift, she comes in early and gets dressed in uniform. Then the officers on her shift are briefed by a sergeant for about thirty minutes, and beats are assigned based on seniority.

Julianne is responsible for all the freeways, state and county roads, and unincorporated area roads within her beat. After checking her patrol car to make sure that she has all the equipment that she needs, she drives her beat looking for disabled vehicles, debris, and traffic violators and answering calls for service. No two days are alike.

A Dream Job. For Julianne, one of the most appealing aspects of being a state highway patrol officer is the freedom that it offers. No one is looking over her shoulder, and she can largely go where she wants. In addition, she especially appreciates the camaraderie with the others on this job. Of course, there is a component of danger; however, she has been so thoroughly trained that her responses are automatic.

Firefighters on the Move

Firefighters have to be ready to respond immediately to a fire or any other emergency that arises. Drivers of fire engines and the paramedic vehicles of fire departments must acquire special skills in order to get through traffic as fast as possible. Their actual time on the move is extremely important because the faster they get to an emergency, the better the outcome is likely to be. Besides driving trucks to emergency situations, drivers—who are called engineers—also make inspection tours, checking for potential fire hazards, as well as trips to a variety of stores for supplies needed at the station.

Qualifications and Training

Both in the United States and Canada, applicants for municipal firefighting jobs generally must pass a written exam; tests of strength, physical stamina, coordination, and agility; and a medical examination that includes drug screening. Completion of high school is also usually required. In Canada, the completion of a college program in fire protection technology or a related field may be required, while in the United States, more and more applicants have had some postsecondary education.

Almost every entry-level firefighter in the United States and Canada takes several weeks of training. Typically, this is received at a large departmental training center or an academy. Another option is to be part of an apprentice program in which on-the-job training is given under the supervision of experienced firefighters.

Job Outlook and Earnings

Although prospective firefighters will face keen competition for available job openings, the employment of firefighters is expected to grow faster than the average of all occupations through 2014 in the United States. This is because many volunteer firefighting positions will be converted to paid ones. You will have the best chance to get a position if you have some firefighter education at a community college, have received emergency medical training certification, and are in excellent physical condition. In Canada, your prospects for getting a job as a firefighter are only fair through 2009, as the employment growth rate will likely be below average, and the number of job seekers is likely to match the number of job openings.

The median hourly rate for firefighters in the United States is more than $18, with the middle 50 percent earning between $13 and $25 per hour. In Canada, the average hourly earnings exceed C$24. In both countries, firefighters usually receive benefits that include medical and liability insurance, vacation and sick leave, retirement benefits, and some paid holidays. Protective clothing is almost always supplied.

On the Road in a Fire Truck

Damon Pellegrini is a firefighter in a suburban area that includes hills covered with trees and large areas of dry grass in the summer. Where he lives, securing a position as a firefighter is extremely competitive. Damon actually had an excellent background for getting a job because he was a volunteer firefighter and had gone to paramedic school. At his present station, there is a tiller truck, a regular truck with a three-hundred-gallon water tank, a type-three grass rig, an engine (onboard water supply), and an ambulance. Tiller trucks have metal ladders that can expand like a telescope. They also have two drivers—one in the front and one in the back. The back driver controls the rear wheels of the truck so it can go around corners easily.

For the first six months that Damon was a firefighter, he did not drive. Then he was placed in the driver's seat of an engine for training and trips to the store before he could drive to a fire. He had previously passed a driver-operator test. For each shift at his current station, he is assigned to a particular vehicle. When he drives, he doesn't go through red lights or take risks. Damon describes driving the tiller truck as quite a responsibility—still, he loves driving this truck. It is fifty-three feet long, weighs seventy-three thousand pounds, and carries three firefighters. When he drives this truck, he is also responsible for setting the truck up at the scene of a fire, which includes putting water through the truck and getting the ladder in the right spot.

A Typical Day. There is rarely a day that something doesn't happen at Damon's fire station. Besides responding to calls, the station's firefighters have to check hydrants and do weed abatement checks in the summer and watch for flooding in the winter. Damon's work schedule includes forty-eight hours straight at the station followed by four days off. On a recent day, he was assigned to drive an engine. Most of the day's activities involved housekeeping. He had to buy a new oven, check out equipment, and move the truck to another station to cover calls while those firefighters had training. On that day, there were three ambulance runs but no fire runs. Damon finds satisfaction in his career every day because he knows that he is helping people even though there is a lot of risk in what he does.

Paramedics and Emergency Medical Technicians (EMTs) on the Move

Automobile accidents, heart attacks, drownings, childbirth, and gunshot wounds all require immediate medical attention. It is the paramedics and EMTs who provide this vital attention as they care for or transport the sick or injured to a medical facility. In an emergency, they are dispatched to a scene by a 911 operator. Every emergency that EMTs and paramedics handle involves driving. These careers are a good choice for those who want to combine a career in the medical area and being on the move.

Full-time and part-time paramedics and EMTs work for private and public ambulance services, emergency medical services, and police and fire departments. In some fire departments, like the one Damon Pellegrini works for, all of the firefighters are also paramedics or EMTs. Those driving emergency vehicles must have an appropriate class of driver's license.

Qualifications and Training

Formal training and certification are necessary to become a paramedic or EMT. There are four different levels, ranging from EMT-1 to EMT-Paramedic, with the highest level requiring up to two years of training. States and provinces provide certification or licensure according to the type and length of training, with each level having specific duties that they can perform. Paramedics are the ones able to provide the most extensive prehospital care, while those with EMT-1 certification can only provide basic emergency care at the scene or while transporting patients by ambulance to the hospital under medical direction.

Job Outlook and Earnings

Most EMTs and paramedics work in metropolitan areas. Their employment in the United States is expected to grow much faster than the average for all occupations. Job opportunities are best with private ambulance services, and competition for jobs is most intense in fire and police departments.

The earnings of EMTs and paramedics depend on the employment setting and geographic location. The median annual salary in the United States is more than $25,000 a year. Those who are part of fire or police departments receive the same benefits as police officers or firefighters. In Canada, EMTs and paramedics have median annual earnings of close to C$40,000.

Animal Control Officers on the Move

The term *dogcatcher* does not begin to describe the duties of animal control officers in this fast-growing field. They act as the first line of defense to protect the health and safety of both humans and animals. Animal control officers investigate the mistreatment and abandonment of animals and work with dangerous and unattended animals. Wages depend on the size of the community and its commitment to modern animal control programs. Wages begin at the minimum wage level and increase based upon the control officer's training.

On the Move with an Animal Control Officer

If you choose to be an animal control officer, as Linda Adams did, you can expect to be on the move 80 percent of the time in a van or truck. Before you get this job, however, you must demonstrate that you have a knowledge of animals; a law enforcement background that includes course work in arrest, search, seizure, and citation authority; firearms training; and the ability to drive a big truck. Linda gained these skills through college classes and a previous job as a ranger.

Linda worked for one of the largest counties in California and would easily drive 150 miles in a day as she made from twenty to thirty stops handling the following responsibilities:

- Patrolling for stray animals
- Responding to animal emergencies such as removing animals from hot cars, horses from canals, and rattlesnakes from freeway rest stops
- Answering animal complaint calls (barking dogs)
- Taking care of dog bites
- Investigating animal welfare and cruelty
- Picking up food donations for animal shelters

On the Job. Linda's schedule as an animal control officer was not an easy one. She worked four ten-hour days and every weekend, as well as being on call two nights a week. Typically, her day would begin at 7 A.M., when she and her fellow officers arrived at the shelter and found out what needed to be done immediately. During the day, additional calls would constantly come in for emergencies as well as other animal control problems. By 7:30 A.M., Linda, wearing a law enforcement uniform, a badge, and a name tag, was ready to climb behind the wheel of the one-ton truck that she drove.

During the course of her workday, she would return to the shelter with stray dogs and cats and to the wildlife rescue center with wild animals whenever the cages on her truck were full. This would usually necessitate at least two trips a day. Because stops to handle problems were often quite far apart in the county, this was truly a job for someone who liked to drive. There are often risks involved with this job in which you may be required to subdue and capture animals or deal with very angry people. However, the independence of being out on the road by yourself is a great plus for most road warriors.

For More Information

No matter what career you are researching, you are likely to find valuable information through related professional associations. Here are some associations that you may wish to contact about jobs involved in driving emergency and public safety vehicles.

Police Officers

Canadian Police Association
141 Catherine Street, Suite 100
Ottawa, ON K2P 1C3
Canada
www.cpa-acp.ca

International Union of Police Associations
1549 Ringling Boulevard, Suite 600
Sarasota, FL 34236
www.iupa.org

National Association of Police Organizations
317 South Patrick Street
Alexandria, VA 22314
www.napo.org

Firefighters

International Association of Firefighters
1750 New York Avenue NW, Suite 300
Washington, DC 20006
www.iaff.org

International Association of Firefighters
350 Sparks Street
Ottawa, ON K1R 7S8
Canada
www.iaff.ca

National Fire Academy
U.S. Fire Administration
16825 South Seton Avenue
Emmitsburg, MD 21727
www.usfa.fema.gov/nfa

EMTs and Paramedics

National Association of Emergency Medical Technicians
PO Box 1400
Clinton, MS 39060
www.naemt.org

National Registry of Emergency Medical Technicians
Rocco V. Morando Building
6610 Busch Boulevard
Columbus, OH 43229
www.nremt.org

Paramedic Association of Canada
300 March Road, Fourth Floor
Ottawa, ON K2K 2E2
Canada
www.paramedic.ca

Animal Control Officers

Canadian Federation of Humane Societies
102-30 Concourse Gate
Ottawa, ON K2E 7V7
Canada
www.cfhs.ca

National Animal Control Association
PO Box 480851
Kansas City, MO 64148
www.nacanet.org

CHAPTER EIGHT

Teaching Others to Drive

E very year, millions of teenagers need instruction to learn how to drive cars. Many seniors need refresher courses to strengthen their driving skills, and tens of thousands of new truck drivers require instruction to get commercial driver's licenses. Even race car drivers need instruction in order to be in the winner's circle. And others are interested in learning how to drive motorcycles or do high-performance driving. While teaching these people how to drive does not usually put you behind the wheel, it can keep you on the move. And at times, you will be able to demonstrate your driving skills, especially if you are working with prospective truck drivers, future participants in races, or those trying to become high-performance drivers.

The workplace is diverse for those who wish to teach others to drive. You could be employed at a commercial school or high school teaching teenagers how to drive. Or you could be employed at a company or private school teaching adults how to drive trucks and buses. There is also the possibility of teaching people to race or drive professionally at a high-performance driving school.

Do You Have What It Takes to Teach Driving?

It is a tremendous responsibility to teach people how to be skilled and safe drivers. Successful driver training instructors share certain attributes that allow them to shine in the profession.

Answer the following questions to see if you are like those instructors.

1. Do you like working closely with people? You cannot be a loner in this job.
2. Are you able to assess a person's ability to handle a task? If you can't, you might ask someone to do something that could endanger you and the other person.
3. Can you see what a person needs to do to acquire a certain skill? You must understand the steps involved in learning specific driving skills.
4. Can you give instructions so that they are easily understood and followed? Confused trainees can have accidents.
5. Can you remain calm in tense situations? All driving teachers will face scary moments.
6. Do you like helping others learn new skills? Good instructors love to teach.
7. Are you an organized person? You need to teach driving according to a well-thought-out lesson plan.
8. Are you patient? Students will not learn at the same rate; some require more instruction.
9. Do you have a good driving safety record? You must be concerned about safety in order to teach it.
10. Are you a skilled driver? You cannot teach skills that you do not have.

If you answered yes to most of these questions—and have a good driving record—then a career teaching driving may be one you should explore.

Driver Training Programs for Teens

Teenagers are the largest group taking driver training programs. Before the 1940s and 1950s, most teens learned how to drive from their families or friends. Then many states began to mandate that students receive their driving instruction in high school courses. As school budgets began to shrink and a shortage of teachers occurred in the 1980s, the behind-the-wheel section of the course began to disappear from high schools. Today, the majority of high schools offer only classroom instruction. Therefore, only limited opportunities to be on the move and teach driver education to teens exist in public schools. Most teens learn to drive from commercial schools or community colleges, with a few learning from family members.

Commercial Driver Training Schools

Learning how to drive at a commercial driving school is popular for these three reasons:

1. Many states require the completion of a certain number of hours in a driver's education course before future drivers can apply for a learner's permit or driver's license.
2. Attending a driver's education program can qualify beginning drivers for a reduced insurance rate.
3. Some states require attendance in a course if an individual's driving record indicates that they need a refresher course on the rules of the road.

There are more than eight thousand commercial driver training schools in the United States and Canada. The vast majority of the schools are quite small and have only one to three cars. Once you gain experience as a driver training instructor, there is also the possibility of opening your own school and becoming an owner-instructor, as many instructors have done. The number of hours of classroom and behind-the-wheel instruction time that driving schools offer is based on state or provincial law. The most common pattern is thirty classroom hours and six hours of driving time, with some states requiring as much as ten hours of driving time. Certain states also require students to spend additional time in a training car observing other students drive. Instructors may teach both in the classroom and in cars; however, most concentrate on one area or the other.

Commercial driver training schools need to be approved by the state or provincial department of transportation motor vehicles division to ensure that their courses meet the standards required for issuing licenses to new drivers. Each state or province sets its own requirements.

Qualifications

You must obtain a license in order to be an on-the-road driver training instructor. Depending on the state or province where you wish to work, you typically have to meet the following requirements:

- Be twenty-one years old
- Have a high school diploma or equivalent
- Be fingerprinted for national and state or provincial background checks
- Have a good driving record
- Have no felony convictions
- Complete an approved course in a licensed school
- Pass both written and driving tests administered by the Department of Motor Vehicles

Before you actually begin teaching at a driving school, you can expect the school to give you some on-the-job training.

Working Conditions

The majority of your students will be teenagers; the remainder will be adults, especially those born in other countries. Most states and some Canadian provinces now have graduated licensing for teenage drivers. There are three stages: a supervised learner's period; an intermediate license (after passing the driver test) that limits driving in high-risk situations except under supervision; and a license with full privileges. Depending on the state or province where you work, you may instruct students for six to ten required hours. These hours are divided into increments of one to three hours of instruction at a time.

Whether you are teaching teenagers or adults, what you teach in each session with a student driver is usually spelled out by your driving school. Of course, you must adjust your instruction to the individual drivers as they will not all pick up skills at the same rate. For example, some may need more help with backing up or parallel parking, and a few will need very little instruction.

If you work for a large driving school or a public high school, students will come to the school to begin their lessons. If you work at a small school, you might pick each student up at his or her home in a car provided by the school. You will probably be able to take this car home and drive the car as your own. The only special equipment that it will have is an additional set of brakes and sometimes a steering wheel on the passenger side for the instructor to use, if necessary.

How much you teach depends on whether you are a full-time or part-time instructor. Most teachers are part-timers. Because the majority of your students will be in high school, your work schedule is largely determined by when they are free. Except in the summer, you can expect your workday to begin after 3 P.M. and extend into the evening. You will also most likely work on weekends.

Job Outlook and Earnings

Because the majority of driver training instructors only work on a part-time basis, there is always a good opportunity for licensed instructors to find jobs. Driver training instructors in commercial schools are usually paid by the hour. Only a few are salaried employees. Those who use their own cars may contract for work at more than one school. How much you earn in this job depends greatly on where you live as well as the number of hours you work. The average hourly pay for instructors in the United States ranges from a low of $10 per hour to a high of $17 per hour. In Canada, the range is from C$11 to C$18. You can expect to earn less in a rural area than in a large metropolitan area. Full-time employees may receive health benefits and paid vacations.

The Career Path of a California Driving Instructor of the Year

Before Walter Branch became a driver training instructor, he worked with troubled youth in social service organizations. When he decided to change careers, he knew that he wanted to continue working with young people. He also thought of how he had always enjoyed driving. The possibility of having a career that included both of these elements was realized when he saw an ad for instructors at a large commercial driving school. Before being hired, Walter had to get a state license to become a driver training instructor. The school provided eighty hours of training split equally between classroom and on-the-road instruction that he needed for a license.

As an instructor at this school, Walter's workday was 9 A.M. to 5 P.M. In the morning, he would teach adults, and in the afternoon his students were primarily teenagers. He typically worked weekends and had two days off during the week. After Walter amassed a thousand hours of working with students in the car, he was able to obtain a license to teach driver education in the classroom.

Becoming a Driving School Manager. An opportunity arose for Walter to work as a manager and driver training instructor at a driving school that had five cars and five instructors. In his new job, he also started teaching in the classroom. From this school, he moved to a larger school with twenty cars as an instructor and then became the manager. Besides handling the manager's job, Walter also taught driver education classes in the classroom as well as driver training classes on the road. His many responsibilities included scheduling the other drivers and training all new drivers. Plus, he had to devote time to riding with all the instructors to ensure that they were following the school's driving curriculum. One of the perks of this position was that Walter no longer worked on weekends.

On the Road Instructing Students. Because of his many other responsibilities, Walter was only out on the road with students two or three days a week. Like all the other drivers at the school, he followed a prescribed format in each training session. The first two-hour session was designed to acquaint students with the car. They learned such things as how to read the gauges, adjust mirrors, and operate all accessories. Then Walter took them out on neighborhood streets, where they engaged in such basics as steering, making right and left turns, and backing up. The second session was devoted to freeway driving, while the third was a review of everything they had learned. During this last session, he pretested them to make sure they had mastered all of the skills essential to passing the state driving license test.

In his role as instructor, Walter tries to make his driving sessions very practical. If it is time to fuel the car, the student pumps the gas and washes the windows at the service station. At the end of each session, Walter reviews the student's strengths and weaknesses so the student will know what areas he or she should concentrate on improving before the next session or before taking the state driving test.

Over the years, Walter has had his share of scares. In fact, he doesn't believe that you truly are a driving instructor until you have been scared. He particularly remembers an adult who changed lanes in front of an eighteen-wheeler without his telling her to do so.

Starting His Own Driver Training School. After several years of managing a school, Walter decided that he had the administrative experience to start his own school. His school has five cars—all PT Cruisers. There is one full-time instructor and four part-time instructors, including Walter. His school teaches a considerable number of adults, especially those who have special needs.

Career Satisfactions. Walter is proud that he has driven a million miles and taught tens of thousands of students without ever being involved in an accident. He has found it delightful to work with people who are so eager to learn. Because Walter has taught so many students, he is unable to go anywhere in his community without running into someone he has taught to drive. Walter was named Driving Instructor of the Year by the Driving School Association of California for his expertise as a driving instructor.

Advanced Training Driving Schools

Most drivers are satisfied to learn the basics of driving from commercial schools, high schools, family, or friends in order to obtain a license. Some drivers, however, want to go beyond this—even to becoming race car drivers. High-performance driving schools offer advanced training in driving through such courses as:

- **Highway Survival:** Teaches car handling skills to those who want to become more confident drivers.
- **Defensive Driving:** Teaches drivers, often teenagers, the skills needed to avoid accidents. Stresses car control techniques, including skid control and advanced braking.
- **High-Performance Driving:** Gives drivers advanced training to increase their enjoyment of driving. Offers advanced driving experiences on a racetrack or specially designed course that cannot be obtained on public highways. Lets drivers use their own cars.

- **Road Racing:** This course is for people who want to know what it is like to drive a race car on a track, for those who want beginning or advanced instruction in driving a race car, as well as for experienced racers.
- **Security Driver Training:** Teaches chauffeurs, security personnel, and executives how to detect, avoid, and prevent potentially dangerous situations.
- **Specialty Courses:** Designed to teach stunt drivers and police the skills required in their careers.

High-performance driving schools range in size from the large Bob Bondurant School, which offers a wide variety of courses, to much smaller schools offering a very limited curriculum.

The Bondurant School of High-Performance Driving

More than eighty-five thousand people have taken courses at the Bondurant School. In this group are movie stars, such as Nicolas Cage, Katie Holmes, David Arquette, and Tom Cruise. Athletes, including Mia Hamm, Nomar Garciaparra, and Terrell Owens, have also taken courses, as well as TV personalities Geraldo Rivera, Jimmy Kimmel, and Paris Hilton. Race car drivers, including Al Unser Jr., Terry Labonte, Darrell Waltrip, and Jeff Gordon, have also honed their skills at the Bondurant School. However, most students at the school are simply individuals with a desire to drive like professionals.

The school was started in 1968 by Bob Bondurant, who had been a very successful race car driver. He had grown up with a passion for anything on wheels and was racing motorcycles on dirt ovals by the time he was eighteen. Then he started driving sports cars, winning many races, such as the GT category at the prestigious Le Mans.

Bob's expertise was recognized with awards, including the Corvette Driver of the Year Award. He also raced Formula One cars successfully.

A very serious racing accident in 1967 forced Bob to think about the future. After a short stint as an instructor at another high-performance driving school, he decided to open his own school and use his experience and expert knowledge of driving to teach others. The school is now located outside of Phoenix, Arizona, at the Firebird International Raceway Complex. It has a fifteen-turn, 1.6-mile racetrack designed by Bob for high-performance race driving and advanced driving instruction. There is also an eight-acre pad used for advanced driver training. The school has more than two hundred race-prepared vehicles, sedans, and open-wheel cars.

On the Move with a High-Performance Driving Instructor

Craig Mintzer has a job that would delight any road warrior. As the assistant chief driving instructor at the Bondurant School, he spends much of his time handling such administrative tasks as scheduling courses, designing courses, and special events. However, he also has time to get behind the wheel and demonstrate how to do high-performance driving to students as well as to participate in an occasional race.

A description of how Craig teaches the Grand Prix Road Racing course will help you understand the work of instructors at this high-performance driving school. This particular course is designed for those who have dreamed of driving a race car or are considering a career in professional motor sports. Course graduates are eligible for an SCCA (Sports Car Club of America) Regional License as well as other competition licenses.

The first day of the course begins with the chief instructor giving the students, usually twelve, a walking tour of the facility and a description of how the course works. Then everyone goes into the classroom to learn about the basics of this type of driving, especially the physics involved in road racing, from one of the four course instructors. When this class is over, the students meet their personal instructors—one for every three drivers.

Instruction Days One and Two. Before Craig meets the drivers who are assigned to him, he checks to make sure his personal car is both safe and clean. He begins the lesson with a demonstration drive on the training track. Craig describes this as a ride and a half that shows exactly what the car can do when an expert driver is at the wheel. Then he gives his drivers a demonstration of the skills they should practice first before pulling off the course. At this point, each driver gets into his or her own assigned car after safety instructions. They follow Craig through the course as he shows them what they should be doing. Next, Craig pulls off the course, parks, and monitors how his drivers are progressing before getting into the car of each driver to give them personal instruction. This is definitely the scariest part of being an instructor.

Through the rest of the morning session, the students follow the same program of learning a skill from Craig, following him on the course, and then practicing. After this three-hour driving session, there is a break for lunch and another class before the students return to the course for another three-hour driving session. The pattern for the second day is largely the same, as the drivers continue to learn and practice such fundamentals as braking, skid recognition and recovery, steering, and throttling.

Instruction Days Three and Four. On the third day of instruction, Craig and his drivers move to the 1.6-mile road course, where he slowly introduces the track to them by showing where to brake, accelerate, and turn. He also drives a couple of hot laps. The drivers then get into their own cars and follow Craig through the course to learn the racing line. The rest of this day is spent in practice. Craig rides with each driver and demonstrates what changes they need to make to improve their skills.

On the last day, the drivers actually participate in a race. First, however, Craig shows them how to start and obey flags. When Craig teaches more advanced courses, he and the other instructors actually race against professional drivers. They are proud to say that they have never lost one of these races. This clearly demonstrates the expertise of Bondurant instructors.

Craig's Career Path. Craig really enjoyed his very successful racing career. He was a two-time National Karting Champion and Formula Ford North American National Champion. While racing full-time, Craig began to instruct part-time to fill the time between races. Then he became involved in a family business for about ten years. However, he still liked to be on the move, so he returned to driving as an instructor. Today, he is the assistant chief driving instructor at Bondurant. As far as his racing career goes, he still races occasionally, mainly in six-hour endurance races.

Craig has found a lot of satisfaction in his career as an instructor—especially in teaching young people to drive. He believes that he may have given some of them skills that could save their lives.

Jim Russell Racing Schools

Since 1957, Jim Russell Racing Schools have been training racing champions. Included in the curriculum is a full spectrum of open-wheel racing schools, karting schools, performance driving schools, and corporate adventures. The school caters to both novice and professional drivers. Instructors at this school have had the opportunity to teach such world-class racers as Danny Sullivan, Emerson Fittipaldi, and Tony Stewart, as well as kids wanting to learn karting and adults interested in a course on highway survival. Most of the twenty-five instructors work part-time and are off racing or doing something associated with racing the rest of the time. Some serve as personal coaches to individuals learning how to race. They work with these racers for a day or two before a race or during a race weekend.

The Youngest Instructor. Champion racers begin racing and winning when they are quite young. J. R. Hildebrand is only nineteen years old today and a recent high school graduate. He attended the Jim Russell Racing School, where he started in 125cc TAG kart racing and competed in the school's "Arrive and Drive" series, taking four wins in six races and the championship. Then three years ago, he took the school's overall racing championship. With the support of the school, J.R. competed in the Pacific F2000 Championship in 2005 and took two wins. In 2006, he was the overall champion in the Cooper Tires Formula Ford 2000 Championship. He has recently moved to Indianapolis to be closer to his team and for training. However, this already successful racer will teach a variety of school programs when his racing schedule permits.

BSR, Inc.—a Different Instructional Focus

BSR has been conducting specialty driving training since 1977. The training site is located in the Shenandoah Valley, seventy-one miles from Washington, D.C. The training site has three paved-road circuits, one dirt-road circuit, one off-road training arena, seven firing ranges, two skid pads, and ten classrooms. It is a leader in vehicle antiterrorist training—instructing a great range of drivers, including staff drivers, military attachés, senior officers, special agents, hostage rescue personnel, diplomats, security officers, undercover agents, governmental protective service personnel, and counterterrorist units. Instructors at this school teach courses tailored accurately to clients' varied needs. They teach such things as evasive driving, convoy and motorcade operations, and unimproved and off-road driving.

Truck Driver Training Schools

No one can drive a large truck or a tractor-trailer without some training. In the past, many learned how to drive by riding with other drivers. Today, most drivers pick up the skills needed to drive these vehicles by attending a truck driving school. As an instructor, you have the opportunity to teach at different types of truck driving schools. You could teach driving at a community college or vocational-technical school and be part of a staff that offers a wide variety of courses. There are also private driving schools as well as schools operated by trucking companies.

At each of these schools, the primary course that you should expect to teach is the operation of tractor-trailers. The length of this course is typically more than four weeks, with both classroom instruction and behind-the-wheel practice. Instructors who want to be on the move will opt to teach in the tractor-trailer truck rather than the classroom. Many instructors, however, teach in the classroom as well as on the road.

There is one other type of truck driving school where you could teach. These schools are operated by major trucking companies for their newly hired drivers who already know how to drive a tractor-trailer. They are designed to hone their employees' driving skills as well as introduce them to the business side of handling all the paperwork required by the company.

When you investigate job opportunities as an instructor, you should also consider whether or not the school offers entry-level courses that are certified as meeting the minimum standards of the Professional Truck Driver Institute (PTDI). If so, you know that you will be teaching a course that meets the standards set by the industry in curriculum, instruction, behind-the-wheel time, and reputation with funding sources and the industry itself. A list of these schools can be found at www.ptdi.org.

Being an instructor at a truck driving school will not give you a great number of hours behind the wheel. However, it will give you the immense satisfaction of helping students take the first steps in becoming professional drivers. It is, therefore, an excellent career choice for road warriors. Many instructors do get considerable time behind the wheel by working part-time as instructors and part-time as truck drivers.

Job Outlook

Truck driving schools are growing faster than ever to meet the demand for new drivers. Old schools are expanding, and new schools are emerging. Most new truck drivers will need to attend a truck driving school in order to learn how to operate tractor-trailers. In fact, most trucking companies require new drivers to have passed entry-level tractor-trailer driving courses. Plus, the Federal Motor Carrier Safety Administration requires training for entry-level drivers in the following four areas: driver qualification, hours of service, driver wellness, and whistle-blower protection. In addition, even experienced drivers need some schooling to learn how to handle each company's nondriving side of trucking, from paperwork to dealing with customers. Therefore, the need for instructors in this very small career area should remain high, especially in new and expanding schools.

SAGE Truck Driving Schools

SAGE has more than thirty driving schools nationwide and has been providing top-quality, comprehensive professional truck driving experience to thousands of students for almost twenty years. SAGE's truck driving instruction is conducted on a private, one-on-one basis on the road. There is never more than one student in a truck. SAGE believes that you learn to drive by driving, not by watching others drive.

To become an instructor at this school, you must have at least five years of successful truck driving experience and a health card, as well as have a commercial driver's license and a good safety record. There are job opportunities for both full-time and part-time instructors. Once someone is hired as an instructor, he or she participates in a week-long orientation program observing classroom and in-truck instruction. It is also necessary to become well-acquainted with the prescribed curriculum for different courses.

What Is Taught. The schools offer a wide variety of truck driving programs to meet the needs of students and employers.

Each training program is patterned after the U.S. Department of Transportation's Proposed Minimum Standards for Training Tractor-Trailer Drivers. SAGE's basic program is designed to exceed the entry-level truck driver certification standards set by the Professional Truck Driver Institute. These are considered the highest national standards for truck driving schools in the country.

The most popular SAGE program is TTD150. It meets the needs of students with no prior knowledge or experience in truck driving, giving them the knowledge and practical skills necessary to become an entry-level over-the-road truck driver. The program consists of 150 hours of instruction, made up of 106 hours in the classroom and 44 one-student-per-truck driving hours conducted over four to five weeks.

On the Move with a TTD150 Instructor

Before Steve Ingraham became an instructor, he was a trainer for a year. Trainers are experienced truck drivers who alternate driving on the road with inexperienced drivers for six to eight weeks. At SAGE, Steve teaches both the classroom and driving parts of TTD150. In the classroom, he teaches the basics of driving a tractor-trailer, including all the regulations that must be followed. When he and a student go on the road in a tractor with a trailer, Steve first shows the student such things as how to double-clutch and turn corners. Then the student practices these skills on out-of-town roads with low to moderate traffic. The goal is for students to do better each day as they learn new skills, such as skid control and backing. Students may learn very fast if they have some skills driving trucks. Each session in the truck with a student is usually four hours, and Steve may teach as many as three sessions in a day. His work schedule is typically Monday through Friday. Some sessions are scheduled at night to give students this experience.

Career Advice. For this career, Steve stresses the importance of being able to communicate well with your students. Plus, it is essential to be able to accurately assess your students' skill levels. He loves being an instructor as it gives him a chance to teach a valuable skill to others.

On the Move with a Company Driving School

Instructors at company driving schools are drivers who have proved themselves on the road. During the course of his career, Marty Fortun, an industry-acclaimed driver whose career was described in Chapter 4, has worked as an instructor. Interestingly, Marty did not learn to drive a truck by attending a driving school. Instead, he learned from family members and on the job at a very early age. This confirmed road warrior even had a job hauling cattle before graduating from high school; he kept the job for a year after graduation before entering the army. In the army, Marty was able to spend three years as a truck driver and left as a very experienced driver.

After completing his stint with the army, Marty was eager to find a job as a professional truck driver. He was able to get a job driving with Schneider National Carriers, where his father worked as a driver, and has been with the company ever since. At that time, company drivers had to be twenty-three, and he was only twenty-two. However, the company said an exception would be made if he agreed to team with his father.

Because of his great aptitude for truck driving, Marty was given his own truck after just three months of team driving. Then, he spent the next two years driving a refrigerated truck on a local route in California.

A Job as a Training Engineer. At the age of twenty-four, Marty became the youngest training engineer that Schneider National

Carriers had ever had who had not attended a driving school. New drivers would attend the Schneider school and then complete their preparation for a career with the company by driving on the road with a training engineer. Marty especially enjoyed this job because the drivers were so eager to get into trucking. He would go out on the road with them, and while they drove he would train them in such things as log writing and trip planning. He would also explain how to handle different situations on the road.

Working as an Instructor. After working as a training engineer for a year, Marty became an instructor at the company's driving school. His job was to hone the actual driving skills of new drivers. On the first day, he would always take students on a demonstration drive so they could see good driving techniques as well as clearly see that he was an experienced driver who knew how to do what he would be teaching them. Then Marty would relinquish the wheel and begin teaching the drivers the basic skills that they would need. This training was done at both the company facility and on the roads around Green Bay, Wisconsin. Part of his time as an instructor was spent working on the skid pad teaching students how to handle skids. The pad had a special surface that became very slippery when water was sprayed on it. He would teach the students both how to get out of skids and how to avoid skidding. When a trailer begins to come around, the driver cannot feel it. Marty had to teach his students to use their mirrors when they were in situations where the truck could jackknife. During the one year that Marty worked at this job, the school would check periodically that he was teaching what they wanted him to teach.

For More Information

To learn the names and locations of driver training schools in your state or province, contact:

Driving School Association of the Americas, Inc.
Communications Office
3090 East Gause Boulevard, Suite 425
Slidell, LA 70461
www.thedsaa.org

For a career as a driving instructor, you can find helpful information about safe-driving courses from:

National Safety Council
1121 Spring Lake Drive
Itasca, IL 60143
www.nsc.org

For a career as an instructor at a truck driving school in the United States or Canada, look at the list of PTDI-certified schools at www.ptdi.org. Career opportunities at high-performance driving schools can be investigated by calling the schools or visiting their websites.

CHAPTER NINE

More Jobs Behind the Wheel

Some people are road warriors—they enjoy each minute they are driving, whether it is on a country road or an interstate. The purpose of this book is to give you ideas about careers that will let you be on the move for most of your workday. Of course, there are still more careers than are covered in this book. You may have to be creative to discover them. You will find it easier if you look around while you are driving down the road for drivers who are at work behind the wheels of their vehicles. Immediately, you will observe highway patrol officers, ambulance drivers, concrete mixer drivers, and moving van drivers. Also, try browsing through an occupational handbook and consider how much driving is involved in different careers. Do the same thing while reading want ads in newspapers or visiting employment sites on the Web.

Here are a few more careers that would be perfect for those who want to spend their working days on the move.

Pizza Delivery Drivers

Reen Suders is a delivery driver for a small pizza shop in Columbia City, Indiana. On a busy day, she spends almost all of her shift on the road getting pizzas to customers as quickly as possible. She may drive as much as eighty to a hundred miles each day. This road warrior also gets to meet many people, which makes this job a lot of fun for Reen.

A typical shift begins with Reen getting a driver's money bag from the store manager. She is responsible for the money in the bag, plus any money she collects from customers she delivers to. Pizza deliveries are dispatched through a computerized order-taking program. Reen checks the computer to see if any orders are ready to go or coming up soon. She checks each order she delivers to be sure all items ordered by the customers are in the pizza delivery bag. When everything is correct, she assigns the order to herself on the dispatch computer and she is ready to hit the road.

It is important to get the order to the customer quickly so the pizza is hot when it gets to them. Just as important is to drive safely. Reen is careful to obey speed limits and traffic signs and signals and to drive courteously. When she arrives at the customer's address, she must collect money and be sure the customer receives everything on the order. Then it is back on the road, either to the next delivery point or back to the store to get another delivery.

Reen has a good knowledge of the streets and roads in the county, but sometimes she refers to a computerized mapping system in the store for exact address locations. She also uses the mapping system to plan her route if she is making more than one delivery. This helps her get from one delivery point to the next as quickly as possible.

When Reen is not making deliveries, she helps with other duties. She makes pizzas and other food, takes orders at the register or on the phone, helps customers who walk into the store, and helps pack up orders being delivered by other drivers. Reen also helps with cleaning duties, including doing dishes, sweeping and mopping floors, taking out the trash, or cleaning food prep areas.

At the end of her shift, Reen counts the money she collected from the customers and turns it in to the manager. In addition to her hourly wage, she earns tips. Some days the tips are really good; other days they're not so good. She does get a portion of a flat delivery fee charged to the customer, which helps pay for her fuel.

Material-Moving Operators

Imagine driving a vehicle with tires that are almost twelve feet high and having to climb a ladder to enter the cab. This is the vehicle that Alysa Dutton drives every day on the job as she hauls dirt from an open-pit coal mine to a dump that actually refills previously mined areas. Her vehicle is commonly described as being about the size of a two-story house. When the bed of this giant dump truck is raised to remove dirt, it is fifty feet up in the air. Alysa is not the only woman driving such a mammoth-size truck; several other women have similar jobs at the mine. While Alysa usually drives dirt trucks, she also drives the same size coal trucks and occasionally much smaller water trucks that are used to keep down the dust.

In order for coal to be removed from this open-pit mine in Wyoming, layers of dirt that cover the coal must first be removed. The dirt is hauled away by six of these giant trucks so that the coal, also hauled in the same size trucks, can be taken to a hopper where it is crushed. Dirt truck drivers, like Alysa, are now driving down six benches, or levels, to reach the current work area. They travel on dirt roads wide enough for two of these trucks to pass. For Alysa, the journey from the spot where a huge shovel places three buckets (240 tons) of dirt in her dump truck to where she dumps it is a distance of one to two miles. She makes this trip about seventy times in a day. This is certainly a job for those who want to be on the move, as Alysa only stops driving for seventy seconds to have the truck loaded and again when the dirt is dumped, except for breaks.

You don't need a license or special classes to drive one of these giant trucks. The only classes that Alysa attended were safety and hazard training. She learned to drive by riding in the cab with an experienced driver and then driving with her mentor driver in the cab until she was ready to solo.

Career Pluses and Minuses

The cab of Alysa's giant dump truck is designed to make her job pleasant. Her seat has springs so she has a comfortable ride over the dirt roads, and she has a radio and cassette player as well as air conditioning. Because the mine operates 365 days a year, twenty-four hours a day, Alysa works twelve-hour shifts, rotating between day and night. She works four days, has seven off, then works four nights followed by three off, then three days followed by one off, and finally three nights with three off before starting the same work schedule all over again. While Alysa finds it difficult at times to switch from working days to nights, she really likes having seven days off at a stretch, which can be extended to fourteen if she takes a week's vacation.

The downside to this job is the monotony involved in doing the same thing over and over at as fast a pace as possible. However, Alysa has learned how to best use her seventy seconds of free time when the truck is being loaded. She has managed to read a lot of books in these short segments of time and exercise with the dumbbells she carries with her in the cab. When she has to wait for the truck in front of her to unload, she uses the truck's ladder as her own stair-step exerciser. Alysa firmly believes that you must be able to entertain yourself in order to enjoy this job, which offers excellent pay and benefits.

Sales Representatives

Bill Haas is a sales representative for an engineering firm that sells sensors to car and automotive accessories manufacturers to use in their plants. While Bill's job is a sales job, it is also one that necessarily involves considerable time on the road, as he visits plants throughout the state of Indiana to make calls on engineers and maintenance people. In a typical year, he travels between twenty-five thousand to thirty thousand miles and is able to spend most nights at home.

Few people realize how many car and automotive accessories plants there are in Indiana. Bill regularly makes sales calls on twenty plants and will visit some every other week. His day may begin as early as 5:30 A.M., when he leaves home to call on a nearby plant by 6 A.M. Once he gets to a plant, his visit may last from forty-five minutes to half a day or more. Some plants are so large that it takes him considerable time even to find the right people to talk to about his company's products. When Bill visits plants close to his home, he obviously does not spend as much time on the road. However, there are many days in which half of his workday is spent on the road. As he drives from plant to plant, Bill enjoys listening to sports on the radio. However, his road time is also business time, as he talks on his cell phone to the office and makes appointments for plant visits.

The Car as an Office

Sales representatives have to show their products to prospective buyers, so Bill carries samples in the car. When he leaves the car to visit a plant, he loads a case with items from the stock of supplies filling the trunk and backseat of his car. There is a milk crate of catalogs and another with literature about products that will be in the next catalog. There are boxes of all kinds of giveaways, including hats, pens, pencils, and pocketknives, for the people he visits in the plants to keep his company name visible. Within the car, Bill also has such office equipment as a BlackBerry, planner, hands-free cell phone, and pager. His car is truly equipped so that it is a mini-office for him.

Career Advice

If you choose a career as a sales representative, Bill wants you to realize that this is not a structured job. You make your own schedule, and it is up to you to decide what time you start to work and how many calls to make in a day. There is also the possibility of working long hours to get a half day free. And, of course, if you have a job like Bill's, you must enjoy working on the road instead of in an office. He only spends one day a week in the office. This is Bill's first job, and he thinks it is an excellent one because it lets him see what role so many people play in the manufacture of cars and automotive accessories.

Marketing Service Representatives

Far more occupations than you probably ever imagined require employees to spend more than half of their time in travel. Nevertheless, these occupations exist in almost every industry. Dustin Crandall, a marketing service representative for a large heavy-equipment manufacturer, has one of these jobs. He spends half of his work time in a car traveling to dealerships in Connecticut, New York, and New Jersey for his company. Dustin's job is to make sure that the dealers are able to correct any defects in material and workmanship or failures that a machine may have. He represents the company and acts as a liaison in communications between the dealerships and company headquarters.

Since Dustin divides his time between five dealerships, he must travel two or three days a week. Depending on the distance, he often stays overnight in a hotel. With this type of travel schedule, Dustin is only in his office one or two days a week. Therefore, he always takes a laptop and cell phone with him so that he can work while on the road and at night in hotels. Most of the work that Dustin does at night involves downloading e-mails and checking his phone messages. There have been some occasions that Dustin has been out of the office for entire weeks on the road. He tries to schedule his trips so that he can be in the office at least one day a week. This gives him the opportunity to get caught up on outstanding issues, report any new problems, and answer questions through e-mail and on the phone.

Since most of Dustin's travels are by car, the company provides him with a company car. It also pays for all his expenses while traveling as well as all expenses associated with the car, including the cost of gas, oil changes, tolls, maintenance and repairs, and even car washes. The only charges that Dustin incurs on the car are when he drives it for his own personal use. Then the company charges him a small fee for each mile he drives. This road warrior likes the advantages of having a career that not only lets him have a company car, but also lets him determine his own traveling schedule. For someone to choose a career like Dustin's, they should like traveling, solving problems with products, and negotiating with others.

Developmental Therapists

Laurie Crider is an early intervention developmental therapist. She teaches parents of disabled children how to play with their children so they may reach their full potential. She works with children from newborn to age three. Laurie travels to the child's home or day-care site in order to provide the service in their natural environment. This road warrior visits three to six homes per day and can travel as much as four hundred miles per week. Her service area covers four rural counties in northeast Indiana. The agency she works for requires her to carefully plan her therapy sessions throughout the week to keep mileage charged to the agency at a minimum. This can be challenging when she also has to work around the schedules of several busy families needing service.

Her vehicle is her main office. She carries three or four bags of toys, a laptop, a cell phone, and report forms with her from visit to visit. Being in the car does have its drawbacks. Laurie says there is a lot of alone time as she travels from home to home, and she has to travel in all types of weather. In addition, she does put a lot of miles on her vehicle, which is her own, and she has high car insurance rates.

Despite the drawbacks, there are many positive things, including meeting a lot of great people and forming strong bonds with the families she serves. Her job is never boring because every day is different. Laurie has a lot of independence as a developmental therapist. She helps parents decide on goals for the child and then she determines what toys and activities will help the child reach those goals.

When Laurie gets to a home, she takes in the bag of toys that she will use with the child. She spends time talking with parents about progress they or the child has made since her last visit. Then she gets on the floor with the child and plays. Parents are an important part of the therapy, so they are present, which encourages development and growth to continue after Laurie finishes her session. At the end of each session, she goes over activities the parents can do with the child until Laurie returns for the next therapy session. Then it is back on the road for her next appointment.

The time between appointments is often very close. She usually has just enough time to complete reports from the previous session and travel to the next. While driving, she has to deal with distractions like cell phone calls, debris on the road, accidents, and reckless drivers. These are a challenge for any road warrior. If she has a new family scheduled, she must double-check directions. She often has to use a map, or she uses a computerized mapping system to be sure she knows exactly where it is she needs to go.

To qualify to be a developmental therapist, you need a four-year degree related to education or special education. Therapists must attend state training sessions throughout the year and must be credentialed every year. Laurie has been a developmental therapist for nearly ten years. She loves the independence involved with the job and enjoys helping children and their parents. Laurie is a true road warrior since she loves to drive and is glad she is "not stuck in a cubicle all day long!"

Meter Readers

On the job as a meter reader for a utility company, Ross Bellow drives as much as twenty thousand miles in a year. He isn't always driving in his car from meter to meter, as he walks some of his twenty-one routes. Also, on some of his routes, he drives to a certain point and then walks a circle before returning to his car. Nevertheless, this is a job that involves a lot of driving. Ross's driving routes vary from twenty to forty-five miles in length.

At each stop, Ross reads the meter in seconds and enters the information in a handheld computer. What takes the most time in this job is accessing the meters on some of the routes. They can be under manhole covers, in backyards, and even on roofs. Plus, there is always the ever-present danger of running into unfriendly dogs and the discomfort of working in bad weather.

On a typical day, Ross arrives at the utility office at 6:30 A.M. and then drives to the start of his route. He is expected to read all the meters on his route, which he always does. By 3 P.M., he is usually able to be back at the utility office to turn in the computer. As a meter reader, he is paid by the hour, uses his own car, and receives a car allowance.

While this is a good job for individuals who want driving to play an important role in their workdays, it is also one that is headed toward extinction. When the technology is perfected, meters will be read remotely by computers that have been sent the data over phone lines.

Security Guards

Security guards can work in one location or be assigned to mobile patrol work. Road warriors will, of course, be interested in those jobs that require security guards to drive from location to location and conduct security checks. Typically, patrol guards are assigned to either a residential or a commercial area, such as a shopping center or business park. Most wear uniforms provided by the security company and may or may not carry a weapon. They usually drive company cars marked with the name of the security company that employs them. These cars may have yellow patrol lights and a spotlight. In order to communicate with the company dispatcher, police, fire department, and wreckers, they use cell phones or radios.

Patrol guards need to be very observant. In residential areas, they are looking for unfamiliar cars, criminal activity, and residents with problems. While residential guards most often drive through assigned neighborhoods at night, guards working in business areas typically are employed on a twenty-four-hour basis. Not only do these guards watch for criminal activity, they are also concerned with such things as traffic and the functioning of stoplights and lawn sprinklers. In both residential and business areas, the guards respond to emergency calls.

Throughout the course of their work, security patrol guards check in electronically along their routes at specific locations. This lets the security company know where they are and ensures their safety. Another task of the guards is to write comprehensive reports of any incidents that occur on their shifts.

Armored Car Guards

Armored cars are very distinctive and easily recognizable vehicles. You have probably seen them on the road as well as stopped to make deliveries and pickups. The driver of the vehicle as well as the accompanying guard or guards are on the move most of the day, so this is truly a job for road warriors. At the same time, this job can be extremely hazardous. When guards are out of the armored car and transporting money and other valuables to and from banks and businesses, they are vulnerable to robberies. In fact, a number of them have been shot in recent years, so armored car guards usually wear bulletproof vests.

Realtors

Marge Blake-Myers is a very successful realtor who is always one of the top ten salespeople in a company of 125 agents selling residential properties in Northern California. Because Marge doesn't list and sell properties in just one community, she spends a great deal of time in her car. She may even spend an entire day showing homes to just one client. Plus, most clients want to visit prospective homes more than once before they put in a bid. Additional time is spent in her car every Thursday between 9:30 A.M. and 2:30 P.M., when Marge drives to open houses showcasing all the new houses that have come on the market that week. Not only does Marge show homes to buyers, she also visits the homes of clients who want to sell their homes.

While realtors like Marge spend considerable time on the move in their cars, her career is really centered on selling homes. Much of her time is spent in the office doing all the paperwork and negotiations involved in the listing, buying, and selling of properties. If you want a career as a realtor, the first step is to obtain a license. Most states require you to complete between thirty and ninety hours of classroom instruction before taking the licensing test, which includes questions on basic real estate transactions and laws affecting the sale of properties. Once you have a license, you may either work for yourself, as two-thirds of all realtors do, or work for a real estate firm. This is one job in which you are at the beck and call of your clients. Expect to work nights and on weekends and more than fifty-hour weeks in order to be a successful realtor.

The demand for realtors is very sensitive to swings in the economy. During periods of declining economic activity and tight credit, the volume of sales and the resulting demand for realtors fall. Nevertheless, this is a career in which the highest 10 percent of realtors earn more than $92,000 a year.

····················

Drag Racers

Tony Schumacher's profession is drag racing. While he has had other jobs to supplement his income, racing has always been his career. Driving is definitely in Tony's blood, as his father was a drag racer, and he can't remember when he wasn't going to tracks. As soon as the local drag strip opened in the spring after his sixteenth birthday, he was there driving a 1986 Trans Am. Then for the next two years after completing high school, Tony raced a 1969 Chevelle that his dad and two friends worked on with him. At that time, he had no idea what his future in racing would be. He did know that he was having fun and going very fast for an eighteen-year-old, doing a quarter mile in ten seconds.

At nineteen, Tony went to the Skip Barber Racing School and learned to drive Formula Fords. After road racing for one year, he had to choose which way his racing career would go: road racing or drag racing. Tony opted for drag racing and started driving a super-comp dragster in competition while attending college. Next, he was asked to drive an Odyssey jet dragster, an exhibition car, which he did for two years. Then, he decided that he wanted to return to competition and bought an alcohol funny car that he and his friends constantly worked on to maximize its speed. A blower explosion totaled this car, and Tony was hired by the Peake brothers to drive a dragster in the fastest class. His success was immediate—he finished second in his first race.

In 1999, Tony's father obtained a new sponsorship for him. Since then, he has won the Winston Championship and finished number two in points in 2000. Tony has become a top drag racer in the United States and no longer needs to work at any job but racing.

While races only take a few seconds, the rest of his time is devoted to testing the car and working with the mechanics to make it go even faster. They have been quite successful. Tony was the first driver to ever run 330.23 miles per hour in 1999. Tony is in his early thirties and plans to continue this career into his fifties.

Career Advice

If you want to be a drag racer, Tony feels it is imperative to surround yourself with the right people and to pay attention to their advice. He also points out that you should not race on streets, which is not only dangerous but doesn't teach you how to race. Tony advises you to go to the track, where race people will help you get started in this career.

. . . .

Indy Racers

So many race car drivers have similar backgrounds. Like Tony, Steve Chassey's father had been involved in racing, and he fondly remembers summer vacations driving across the country and stopping along the way to see races. With this background, Steve knew from an early age that he wanted to be a race car driver. He began to fulfill his dream at age seventeen by racing a stock car, which he had built, on quarter-mile paved tracks. In his very first race, he qualified high enough to make the feature race. Steve went to college but did not stay long because his racing career was taking off.

At the start of his career, Steve always worked other jobs. A stint in Vietnam, however, interrupted his career before it really started. When he returned, he began racing sprint cars and also midget cars.

At this time, he was working in his own auto repair body shop during the day and on his car at night and racing throughout California on the weekend. Steve met with considerable success in sprint car racing and was named Rookie of the Year in California.

From California, Steve moved to the Midwest with the car that his father had purchased for him before Vietnam. Although he had done well with the car in California, it did not have the quality of other cars in the Midwest, where racing was more professional. He began to work for Gary Bettenhausen, a well-known Indianapolis 500 racer, building race cars while at the same time driving sprint and championship dirt cars. By now, he had done well enough in racing that he was receiving offers to drive cars and was able to ask owners for a ride. Steve was paid for racing in the same way as other drivers—the owners gave him 40 percent of what a car earned in a race or 50 percent if he won the race.

The Indianapolis 500

After several years, Steve was able to support himself through racing and doing TV commentary on racing. Besides racing sprint and championship dirt cars, he began to race Indy cars. It is not easy to qualify for the Indianapolis 500. First, Steve had to practice in Indy cars and race at other tracks before he even attempted to enter the 500, which has been called "the greatest spectacle in racing." He was not too successful initially because his car was substandard. However, with a lot of practice and hints from other drivers, he began to meet with success and was able to take even subpar cars to top-ten finishes. As his driving skills increased, he was able to qualify three times for the Indianapolis 500 and to finish eleventh in one of the races.

Few racers have long careers. As Steve grew older, his reflexes slowed and his desire to race decreased, so he decided it was time to retire. He did not abandon racing entirely. He has since started working in the business of insuring cars, racetracks, and drivers.

Career Advice

Steve advises anyone who wants to drive race cars to follow his or her dream. He believes that the best way to get started is with go-karts and then to move up through more demanding cars and tracks. However, because so many do not get to the top echelon as he did, Steve believes that you need to get a good education in case you are unable to fully realize your dreams. He does regret not completing college, as it would have increased his career options after his racing career was over.

Movers

Carl Freeman is a mover who works as an independent contractor for a large international moving company. He owns his own tractor, and the company furnishes the trailer and assigns him to moving jobs. Carl hires helpers to assist him in loading and unloading the trailer. So besides being a road warrior, Carl also functions as a businessperson.

To keep Carl busy and on the move, the company dispatcher tries to schedule several loading jobs within a central area to fill the trailer. In a typical workweek, Carl may spend the first three days getting the trailer loaded, followed by a few days of driving. Then, he works through the weekend to unload everything before starting the cycle all over again. During a given day, Carl can work up to fifteen hours: ten hours of driving and five hours of physical labor. All of his time must be logged and sent back to the company every day.

The Loading Process

Before Carl begins to load the trailer, he must hire helpers. Upon arriving at a home, Carl greets the home owners and introduces himself. He then asks for a tour of the house and explains the loading procedure.

While the local helpers begin moving prepackaged boxes outside and lining them up on the driveway, Carl goes through the entire house, inventorying the items to be shipped and labeling them with stickers. He also records the condition of each piece carefully, noting any damage. Next, he wraps all the furniture with packing blankets and tape, ensuring that they are well padded for the long ride ahead. Then, Carl works with the helpers to disassemble such bulky items as kitchen tables, pool tables, and headboards.

Once all Carl's work in the house is complete, he begins to load the trailer because he is solely responsible for its contents. In the loading process, he touches every box and piece of furniture in the entire house. Once everything is loaded, Carl completes all the paperwork and reviews it with the home owners. If he has a full load, he begins driving; otherwise, he makes other stops to fill the trailer before taking off.

On the Road and Unloading

Due to the hours that Carl works and the vast distances between locations, he spends about 85 percent of his time away from home. While on the road, he sleeps in his extended cab. It is fully loaded with a microwave, refrigerator, and an air-conditioning unit. Once Carl reaches his destination, he contacts the shippers to verify the unloading date and time. He also hires helpers to assist him in the unloading. At the home, Carl again requests a tour to find out where certain items will go. Unloading then begins. The home owners have a sheet with all the label numbers listed, and they mark off each number when the box or item is unloaded. Once the trailer is unloaded, Carl and his helpers reassemble items and remove packing materials from the home. The job is complete when he goes through the paperwork with the home owners.

Job Qualifications

It is not enough for movers to be road warriors with expert driving skills. They must also have solid people skills that allow them to quickly establish a solid working relationship with home owners and helpers. Since there is a great deal of paperwork that must be filled out and filed, movers need to be organized. Plus, with all the lifting and moving of heavy items, they must be physically strong. Finally, in order to be successful as an independent contractor in the moving industry, you must be willing to work very hard.

An Abundance of Job Opportunities

As children, future road warriors often sit behind the wheel of the family car dreaming of the day when they will be drivers. They also visit fire and police stations and envision themselves behind the wheels of these vehicles. Today, more than ever, there is such a wide variety of careers behind the wheel that road warriors can find careers that suit their special interests—from trucker to bus driver to race driver to mover to highway patrol officer—and keep themselves on the move throughout their workdays. And the picture for careers on the move looks bright in the future. Businesses will always need truckers to haul goods to keep the economy humming. And all people must rely on buses, taxis, vans, and limousines to meet some of their transportation needs. Plus, almost everyone who wishes to drive a vehicle, whether it is a car, truck, bus, or race car, needs some help in mastering the intricacies of driving. In fact, such training is often required by law. The next time you are on the road, look at all the other drivers and observe how many have found careers on the move. You could be one of them!

Checklist for Quality Courses in Tractor-Trailer Driver Training

This checklist is a yardstick for prospective students and others in measuring the quality of a tractor-trailer driver training program. Formal training is the most reliable way to learn the many special skills required for safe truck driving. The more skills that are learned in supervised training, the fewer that need to be learned on the job. Such training is available from private truck driver training schools, public education institutions, and in-house motor carrier training programs. Because of the important role of safety in truck driving, the trucking industry has implemented minimum standards by which to measure training programs. The standards are administered through the Professional Truck Driver Institute (PTDI), a national nonprofit organization sponsored by the trucking industry to advance truck driver training, proficiency, safety, and professionalism to industry standards. It evaluates compliance with thirty-six certification standards, which include administration, curriculum, instructional personnel, training vehicles, instruction, and evaluation. Training institutions voluntarily certify their courses to verify that they are meeting PTDI industry standards. Not all schools have chosen to certify their courses; PTDI-certified courses are currently offered at sixty-four schools in twenty-eight states and

Canada. For an up-to-date listing of schools that offer certified courses, check the PTDI website at www.ptdi.org/schools.

You can use the following checklist to evaluate a course against PTDI standards. PTDI-certified courses meet all of these standards plus a number of others. The checklist is only a brief treatment of the standards by which truck driver training quality is measured. It is not intended to provide an exhaustive treatment of evaluation standards. For the full standards and guidelines, see www.ptdi.org/standards. This checklist is reprinted with permission of the Professional Truck Driver Institute.

COURSE ADMINISTRATION

- Is the course accurately and clearly defined and explained in informational materials on topics such as costs, tuition reimbursement (if any), training provided, equipment used, outcomes, classroom hours, and actual individual driving time? (Is the advertising truthful?)
- Are there clearly stated goals that match the needs of students and the trucking industry?
- Are there clear, written eligibility requirements for students that are followed?
- Must an applicant meet minimum Department of Transportation, state, provincial, federal, and local laws and regulations related to drug screens, age, physical condition, licensing, driving ability, and driving record as stated in the school's admissions policy?
- Are there written policies regarding safety, liability, and rules?
- Do admissions follow written procedures?
- Are enrollment agreements required?

INSTRUCTIONAL PERSONNEL

- Do instructors possess a combination of education and experience that clearly qualify them for their assignments?

- Do driving instructors have at least three years of experience as licensed, successful tractor-trailer drivers with a good driving record?
- Do instructors meet state or provincial requirements, school policy, and Federal Motor Carrier Safety Regulations?
- Do instructors have teaching skills?
- Do instructors have a state or provincial license or permit, if required?
- Are instructors thoroughly trained in the curriculum?
- Are instructors carefully supervised and evaluated?
- Do instructors participate in regular staff development programs?

TRAINING VEHICLES

- Are vehicles in good mechanical condition and appropriate for the activities for which they are used?
- Do they meet safety requirements, contain occupant restraint systems for all occupants, and contain working emergency equipment?
- Are training vehicles comparable in size and power to those used by motor carriers in the area?

CURRICULUM CONTENT

- Does the course outline clearly identify units of instruction, including their sequence, broad purpose, and general content?
- Does instruction cover the subject areas identified by PTDI curriculum and skill standards? (See "Primary Functions/ Duties of a Tractor-Trailer Driver" in the *PTDI Skill Standards for Entry-Level Tractor-Trailer Drivers* and "Minimum Hours of Training & Five Curriculum Units" in *PTDI Curriculum Standard Guidelines for Entry-Level Tractor-Trailer Driver Courses.*)
- Does classroom instruction include the use of aids such as films, displays, textbooks, models, and charts?

- Are instructional materials appropriate for the ability of the trainee, and are they up-to-date?
- Are materials provided to each trainee?

INSTRUCTIONAL TIME

- Does each student receive at least 104 (sixty-minute) hours in combined classroom and lab time? (Lab is instruction that occurs outside the classroom that does not involve actual operation of the vehicle and its components; this includes time on the range under the supervision of an instructor. Observation time does not count as instructional time.) Independent study may be substituted for up to one-third of classroom hours. Independent study is not the same as homework.
- Does each student receive at least 44 (sixty-minute) hours of actual behind-the-wheel time? (This is time with hands actually on the wheel, with at least twelve hours on the range and twelve on the road and the other twenty hours on either.)
- Is the trailer loaded with a minimum of fifteen thousand pounds during at least 25 percent of street instruction time?
- Are night-driving principles taught and practiced, with a minimum of one hour of behind-the-wheel time at night?
- Is the total length of the instructional day, including independent study, not longer than ten hours on average?

CLASSROOM CONDITIONS

- Is the learning environment safe, sanitary, and comfortable?

STUDENT/INSTRUCTOR/TRUCK RATIO

- Does classroom and lab instruction average one instructor for not more than each group of thirty students?
- Is there never more than one instructor to three trucks on the range?

- During driving, is there one instructor per truck and never more than four trainees in the truck?

LESSON PLANS
- Do instructors use lesson plans to guide each session?
- Are students provided with behind-the-wheel lesson driving procedures along with a list of safety rules for street driving?

RANGE CONDITIONS
- Is the range safe and protected from the hazards from other road users?
- Is the range free of obstructions, and does the surface enable the driver to maneuver without loss of control?
- Are there adequate sight lines available to the instructor and trainees?

STREET INSTRUCTION CONDITIONS
- Is driving practiced under various roadway and traffic conditions?

TESTS
- Do written classroom and lab tests assess mastery of a sample of knowledge objectives for each unit of instruction?
- Do range tests assess student proficiency in (a) fundamental vehicle control skills and (b) routine driving procedures?
- Do road tests use routes that permit a broad range of observations, and are they planned in advance?
- Are road tests administered in a standard van or box-type tandem-axle trailer (with minimum length of forty-five feet) and a tractor with a tandem axle?

DISTANCE LEARNING
- If a portion of the classroom/lab instruction is delivered electronically, is there active two-way communication

between instructor and student? Is the student provided with information about technological competence needed, completion requirements, and any additional costs? Must each student take a proctored exam? Does the course begin and end within a specified time frame? May the students review completed lessons at least once at no additional cost prior to the proctored exam?

GRADUATION

- Does a student have to successfully complete the course equivalent to PTDI content and hours, including tests and road tests, before graduation?
- Does a student secure a commercial driver's license before graduation is conferred?

OUTCOMES AND RECORDS

- Are student critiques of the school used in follow-up?
- Are transcripts provided upon request?
- Does each student keep a driver duty status record to document time behind the wheel?
- Do both the student and instructor sign off on the record?
- Are permanent records kept for at least ten years?

To learn the answers to these questions, you may question school personnel, current students or graduates, and motor carriers who hire graduates from the school.

Largest Trucking Companies by Fleet Size

The following carriers in the United States and Canada are the largest by fleet size, listed in order from largest to smallest. They are carriers of general freight, packages and parcels, heavy equipment, motor vehicles, refrigerated products, household goods, petroleum, auto parts, bulk commodities, hazardous materials, chemicals, and other goods transported by trucks. This material is reprinted courtesy of Transportation Technical Services in Fredericksburg, Virginia.

United States

United Parcel Service Trucking
55 Glenlake Parkway NE
Atlanta, GA 30328
www.ups.com

FedEx Express
3610 Hacks Cross Road
Memphis, TN 38125
www.fedex.com

DHL Worldwide Express, Inc.
1200 South Pine Island Road, Suite 600
Plantation, FL 33324
www.dhl-usa.com

Swift Transportation Co., Inc.
PO Box 29243
Phoenix, AZ 85038
www.swifttrans.com

Schneider National Carriers, Inc.
PO Box 2545
Green Bay, WI 54306
www.schneider.com

J. B. Hunt Transport Services, Inc.
615 J. B. Hunt Corporate Drive
Lowell, AR 72745
www.jbhunt.com

Greatwide Logistics Services
12404 Park Central Drive, Suite 300S
Dallas, TX 75251
www.greatwide.com

Roadway Express, Inc.
PO Box 471
Akron, OH 44310
www.roadway.com

Werner Enterprises, Inc.
PO Box 45308
Omaha, NE 68145
www.werner.com

United Van Lines, Inc.
One United Drive
Fenton, MO 63026
www.unitedvanlines.com

Yellow Transportation, Inc.
PO Box 7270
Shawnee Mission, KS 66207
www.yellowroadway.com

Landstar Carrier Group
13410 Sutton Park Drive South
Jacksonville, FL 32224
www.landstar.com

Con-Way Freight, Inc.
110 Parkland Plaza
Ann Arbor, MI 48103
www.con-way.com

U.S. Xpress Enterprises, Inc.
4080 Jenkins Road
Chattanooga, TN 37421
www.usxpress.com

Ryder Integrated Logistics
11690 Northwest 105th Street
Miami, FL 33178
www.ryder.com

Crete Carrier Corporation
400 Northwest Fifty-Sixth Street
Lincoln, NE 68528
www.cretecarrier.com

Estes Express Lines, Inc.
3901 West Broad Street
Richmond, VA 23230
www.estes-express.com

Allied Systems, Ltd.
2302 Parklake Drive, Building 15, Suite 600
Atlanta, GA 30345
www.alliedholdings.com

Velocity Express, Inc.
One Morningside Drive North, Building B
Westport, CT 06880
www.velocityexp.com

Old Dominion Freight Line, Inc.
500 Old Dominion Way
Thomasville, NC 27360
www.odfl.com

Atlas Van Lines, Inc.
1212 St. George Road
Evansville, IN 47711
www.atlasworldgroup.com

Allied Van Lines
PO Box 988
Fort Wayne, IN 46801
www.alliedvan.com

R+L Carriers
600 Gillam Road 271
Wilmington, OH 45177
www.rlcarriers.com

ABF Freight System, Inc.
PO Box 10048
Fort Smith, AR 72917
www.abfs.com

Averitt Express, Inc.
PO Box 3166
Cookeville, TN 38502
www.averittexpress.com

Quality Distribution, Inc.
3802 Corporex Park Drive
Tampa, FL 33619
www.qualitydistribution.com

Universal Truckload Services, Inc.
11355 Stephens Road
Warren, MI 48089
www.goutsi.com

Covenant Transport, Inc.
PO Box 22997
Chattanooga, TN 37422
www.covenanttransport.com

Comcar Industries
PO Drawer 67
Auburndale, FL 33823
www.comcar.com

Knight Transportation, Inc.
5601 West Buckeye Road
Phoenix, AZ 85043
www.knighttransportation.com

Mayflower Transit
One Mayflower Drive
Fenton, MO 63026
www.mayflower.com

Central Transport International
12225 Stephens Road
Warren, MI 48089
www.centraltransportint.com

CRST International, Inc.
PO Box 68
Cedar Rapids, IA 52406
www.crst.com

Penske Logistics, Inc.
PO Box 563
Reading, PA 19603
www.penskelogistics.com

North American Van Lines, Inc.
PO Box 988
Fort Wayne, IN 46801
www.navl.com

C. R. England, Inc.
4701 West 2100 South
Salt Lake City, UT 84120
www.crengland.com

Interstate Distributor Co.
PO Box 45999
Tacoma, WA 98448
www.intd.com

Celadon Trucking Services, Inc.
9503 East Thirty-Third Street
Indianapolis, IN 46235
www.celadontrucking.com

Saia Motor Freight Line, Inc.
11465 Johns Creek Parkway, Suite 400
Johns Creek, GA 30097
www.saia.com

Heartland Express, Inc.
901 North Kansas Avenue
North Liberty, IA 52317
www.heartlandexpress.com

Ruan Transport Corp.
PO Box 9319
Des Moines, IA 50306
www.ruan.com

Southeastern Freight Lines
PO Box 1691
Columbia, SC 29202
www.sefl.com

Marten Transport, Ltd.
129 Marten Street
Mondovi, WI 54755
www.marten.com

USA Truck, Inc.
3200 Industrial Park Road
Van Buren, AR 72956
www.usa-truck.com

Prime, Inc.
2740 North Mayfair
Springfield, MO 65803
www.primeinc.com

CFI/Contract Freighters, Inc.
PO Box 2547
Joplin, MO 64803
www.cfi-us.com

Dart Transit Co.
PO Box 64110
Saint Paul, MN 55164
www.dartadvantage.com

Gainey Transportation Services
6000 Clay Avenue
Grand Rapids, MI 49548
www.gaineycorp.com

AAA Cooper Transportation
1751 Kinsey Road
Dothan, AL 36302
www.aaacooper.com

Kenan Advantage Group
4895 Dressler Road
Canton, OH 44718
www.kenanadvantagegroup.com

Canada

St. Lambert Transport, Inc.
1950 Third Street
Saint-Romuald, QC G6W 5M6
Canada

Purolator Courier
5995 Avebury Road
Mississauga, ON l5R 3T8
Canada
www.purolator.com

Trimac Transportation Services, Inc.
PO Box 3500
Calgary, AB T2P 2P9
Canada
www.trimac.com

Transport Morneau, Inc.
902 Rue Philipe-Paradis
Quebec, QC G1N 4E4
Canada
www.groupemorneau.com

Day & Ross, Inc.
398 Main Street
Hartland, NB E7P 1C6
Canada
www.dayross.ca

About the Authors

···

Marjorie Eberts and Margaret Gisler have been writing together professionally for thirty-one years. They are prolific freelance authors with more than ninety books in print. Their publications include more than twenty career books, textbooks in language arts and mathematics, advice books for parents, and children's books.

Writing this book was a special pleasure for the authors as it gave them the opportunity to talk to so many road warriors and see how much they enjoyed their jobs. They especially liked riding in eighteen-wheelers, taxis, limousines, and airport shuttles to gain a better understanding of the careers described in this book. The authors truly appreciate the effort that people on the move put into keeping the North American economy moving and making our highways safer for all drivers.

Marjorie Eberts is a graduate of Stanford University, and Margaret Gisler is a graduate of Ball State University. Both received their specialist degrees in education from Butler University. And Margaret Gisler recently received her doctorate in education from Ball State University.